CASABLANCA

As Time Goes By

50TH ANNIVERSARY COMMEMORATIVE

Turner Publishing, Inc.

ATLANTA

The poster art used to sell CASABLANCA captured images that would haunt international filmgoers for half a century. American poster and magazine ad (top, left and right); French and Belgian posters (bottom, left and right). OPPOSITE POSTERS: (Clockwise, from top left) Argentine, French, Finnish, and American. CASABLANCA failed on its initial release in France after World War II but gained greater popularity over time. The picture was shorn of all Nazi reference in post-war Sweden and Germany; during the war, it was banned outright in Ireland.

PUBLISHED BY TURNER PUBLISHING, INC.

A SUBSIDIARY OF TURNER BROADCASTING SYSTEM, INC.

ONE CNN CENTER, BOX 105366

ATLANTA, GEORGIA 30348-5366

COVER ILLUSTRATION BY GARY KELLEY

FIRST EDITION

10 9 8 7 6 5 4 3 2 1

ISBN 1-878685-14-7 (HARDCOVER)

ISBN 1-878685-17-1 (SOFTCOVER)

DISTRIBUTED BY ANDREWS AND MCMEEL

4900 MAIN STREET

KANSAS CITY, MISSOURI 64112

DESIGNED AND PRODUCED ON MACINTOSH COMPUTERS

USING QUARKXPRESS 3.1 AND ALDUS FREEHAND 3.1

COLOR SEPARATIONS BY GRAPHICS INTERNATIONAL, ATLANTA, GEORGIA

PRINTING BY RINGIER AMERICA, NEW BERLIN, WISCONSIN

EDITOR-IN-CHIEF, ALAN SCHWARTZ; EDITOR, LINDA SUNSHINE; COORDINATING EDITOR, LARRY LARSON;

ASSISTANT EDITOR, KATHERINE BUTTLER; COPY EDITOR, MARIAN LORD; PHOTO RESEARCHER, WOOLSEY ACKERMAN;

DESIGN DIRECTOR, MICHAEL J. WALSH; DESIGN/PRODUCTION, KAREN E. SMITH, ELAINE STREITHOF.

Acknowledgments

Like *Casablanca*, this book is the result of a series of happy accidents—accidents that have brought me the help, support, and friendship of a long list of people. Tops on that list are my editor, Linda Sunshine; Michael Reagan, Alan Schwartz, Larry Larson, Michael Walsh, and Kathy Buttler of Turner Publishing; and copy editor Marian Lord, all of whose patience and judgment helped create this book.

I also owe a special debt to my research assistant, Woolsey Ackerman, who located most of the pictures in this book and was invaluable in digging up background information. Aiding us in that area were Linda Maher and Robert Cushman of the Academy of Motion Picture Arts and Sciences' Margaret Herrick Library; Robin Blair Bolger of Eastman House; Leith Adams and Stuart Ng of the Warner Bros. Collection at the University of Southern California School of Cinema-Television; Ned Comstock of the USC Cinema-Television Library's Archive of Performing Arts; Gladys Irvis and Rod Merl at the American Film Institute's Louis B. Mayer Library; Cathy Manolis and Dick May of Turner Entertainment Co.; and the staffs of the State Historical Society of Wisconsin's Collection, Producers Photo Lab, and Camden House Auctioneers, Inc. And a special thanks goes to Roger Mayer, president of Turner Entertainment, who was instrumental in helping gain clearances for some of the material included herein.

Rudy Behlmer and Marvin Paige were generous in sharing their time and resources with me. Scott Benson of Turner Home Entertainment made his own research available to me. Hector Elizondo, Carrie Rickey of *The Philadelphia Inquirer*, Vincent Sherman, and Eleanor Ringel of *The Atlanta Journal-Constitution* took the time to share with me their feelings about the film and, in Mr. Elizondo's case, its second television incarnation. Lee Tsiantis of 20th Century-Fox's Atlanta public relations office was also helpful and supportive. The staff of Turner Broadcasting's Los Angeles PR office—Alison Hill, Joe Swaney, Robyn McPeters, Liz Cain, Joe Lo Cicero, Anthony Masterson, and Alicia Reed helped arrange my research schedule and make my stay in Los Angeles more of a vacation than a working trip.

I also owe a special debt to the friends who have provided emotional support and my colleagues at Turner Broadcasting—particularly Michael Oglesby and Kitsie Riggall.

Finally, the deepest thanks of all go to Lena Tabori, whose help and encouragement played the key role in my transformation from film fan to film writer. Without her, this book would not exist.

Table of Contents

Advertising for CASABLANCA:
Spanish posters (below and
opposite, right); U.S. poster
(opposite, bottom left); and
lobby cards (above, and
opposite, top three).

IMAGINE

For A Moment A Casablanca Where:

• Nightclub owner Ronald Reagan allows himself to be seduced by oomph girl Ann Sheridan in return for the letters of transit she needs to get her lover, Dennis Morgan, to safety in the U.S.;

• Resistance leader Joseph Cotten is killed at the airport by Nazi officer Otto Preminger, leaving Cotten's wife, Hedy Lamarr, free to marry true love George Raft;

• Michelle Morgan asks Ella Fitzgerald to play some of the old songs and the musician obliges with an original piece by film composer Max Steiner.

None of these scenes was ever filmed, of course, but each could have become a part of history had circumstances been slightly different.

If history is viewed as a series of accidents that become fact, then the history of Warner Bros. Production No. 410 is a series of lucky accidents that brought together the perfect script, director, and stars to create the definitive romantic thriller. Had Austrian beauty Hedy Lamarr been available for a loan-out from MGM, she, rather than Ingrid Bergman, would have played Ilsa. Had the play arrived at Warner Bros. a month earlier, before the U.S. entry into World War II, there might have been no interest in bringing it to the screen.

Those involved in *Casablanca's* creation have spoken of the film's chaotic production process. Writer Howard Koch said it was "conceived in sin and born in travail." Several key roles still had not been cast before production began. A final script was not approved until just weeks before shooting was finished, and nobody knew how the picture would end until just before the last scene was shot. After filming was completed, *Casablanca* almost acquired an epilogue and lost one of its most popular elements, the song "As Time Goes By."

But chance, good taste, and sound judgment produced a film that audiences still treasure after fifty years. Financially, the picture has produced rewards far exceeding the $3.5 million in box-office receipts generated during its initial release: it continues to generate profits through theatrical revivals, television syndication, home-video sales and rentals, merchandising agreements, and memorabilia auctions. Artistically, *Casablanca* inspired hordes of imitations and propelled Humphrey Bogart and Ingrid Bergman into the first ranks of superstars. Historically, it stands as a prime example of the kind of timely romantic thriller—one-part cynicism, one-part schmaltz—at which Hollywood excelled during the war years. Culturally, it has become an icon for lost love, devotion to a cause, and a simpler time when right and wrong could be drawn in bold strokes of black and white. And emotionally, the picture has provided the peg on which generations of fans have hung their own ideals and romantic dreams.

This book has been created to celebrate the golden anniversary of one of the most enduring screen favorites of all time. In it are rare production stills, many of them never before reproduced in book form. Also, the text provides insight into how the legend of *Casablanca* came about—from the first words set down on paper by playwrights Murray Burnett and Joan Allison to the most recent honors accorded the picture by fans, critics, and film professionals. Along the way, the story uncovers the truth behind the legends and reveals how the picture's chaotic creation actually helped it remain popular for fifty years.

Movies come, and movies go. People change, as do their values. Trends blossom and fade. But one thing has stayed constant through the past half-century. *Casablanca* remains one of the most popular points of embarkation for dreamers. Everyone wants to be the man in the trench coat or the woman in the white dress, living out the eternal fantasy of romance lost and found and then surrendered in the name of a higher cause. And while that fantasy lives in people's hearts, the world will always welcome lovers, as time goes by.

One Critic Remembers...

Casablanca? You must remember this. Globes spinning. Idealism cloaked as cynicism. Ceiling fans spinning. The Germans wore gray, you wore blue. Roulette wheels spinning. Dooley Wilson sings the blues. Revolver cylinders spinning. Humphrey Bogart, chiaroscuro anti-hero. Airplane propellers spinning. Ingrid Bergman, lust object in white silk; political animal in gray flannel. Letters of transit spinning. Dialogue, like editing, proceeds at Warners' breathless clip. Claude Rains puts a spin on opportunism. Irony, meet patriotism.

I think this is the beginning of a beautiful friendship. Though not the best movie ever, it's the best friend among American films.

—CARRY RICKEY, PHILADELPHIA INQUIRER FILM CRITIC.

PREVIOUS OVERLEAF PAGES: Sam (Dooley Wilson) performs "Knock on Wood" as Rick (Humphrey Bogart) hides the letters of transit beneath the piano's top; Rick bids Ilsa (Ingrid Bergman) farewell in a speech the actors had received only the night before filming.

The sights of Casablanca, including (opposite page, top) the spinning globe seen at the film's beginning; (opposite, bottom) a special-effects shot of the Lisbon plane winging its way past Rick's Café; (counter-clockwise from top right) the bottle of Vichy water Capt. Renault (Claude Rains) tosses aside at the film's conclusion; a police officer reading a teletyped report in the last scene filmed; the opening title card for the film; the cast caricatured in the November 1980 issue of "Esquire"; and, Major Strasser (Conrad Veidt) singing "Wacht Am Rhein" with his fellow officers.

WARNER BROS.
présente
HUMPHREY BOGART
production HAL B. WALLIS
CLAUDE RAINS
Julius J. et Philip G. Epstein et

INGRID BERGMAN
PAUL HENREID

dans

LANCA

SYDNEY GREENSTREET

Mise en scène de Michael CURTIZ
Musique de Max STEINER

OGART · BERGMAN · HENREID

Presented by
WARNER BROS.

Casablanca

CLAUDE CONRAD SYDNEY
RAINS · VEIDT · GREENSTREET ·

A HAL B. WALLIS PRODUCTION   *Directed by* MICHAEL CURTI

CINÉVOG

N° 56
20 MAI
1947

AVEC TOUS LES PROGRAMM

INGRID BERGMAN ET
HUMPHREY BOGART
sont les vedettes du grand film
d'Hal B. Wallis : "Casablanca",
mis en scène par Michael Curtiz.
(Photo Warner Bros.)

NOTRE RUBRIQUE FÉMININE

PREVIOUS OVERLEAF PAGES: The
Vichy police arrest Ugarte (Peter
Lorre) as Rick "sticks his neck out
for nobody"; Poster for French
release of CASABLANCA.

THIS PAGE: (clockwise from top left)
Lobby card; theater program from
CASABLANCA's Czechoslovakian release;
lobby card; shot of Paris café from
the flashback; (center) cover of the
French film magazine "Cinévogue."
OPPOSITE PAGE: (top right) French
poster for CASABLANCA; (left) cus-
tomers at Rick's Café stand to sing
"La Marseillaise"; (bottom right)
Rick and Ilsa drive past the Arc de
Triomphe in the Paris flashback.

A
WARNER
BROS.
PICTURE

CASABLANCA

Why They Don't Make Them Like They Used To

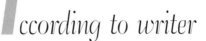

ccording to writer Chuck Ross, not only does Hollywood not make films like it used to, but many in the movie capital wouldn't know a hit if it flew in over the transom. For an "American Film" article he wrote in 1982, Ross retyped the screenplay to "Casablanca," gave it the title "Everybody Comes to Rick's," and submitted it to 217 agencies dealing with writers and film scripts. Of the 85 groups that read the material and responded, only 33 recognized the script; 38 rejected it outright; eight thought it sounded an awful lot like "Casablanca"; three thought they could sell it; and one suggested turning it into a novel.

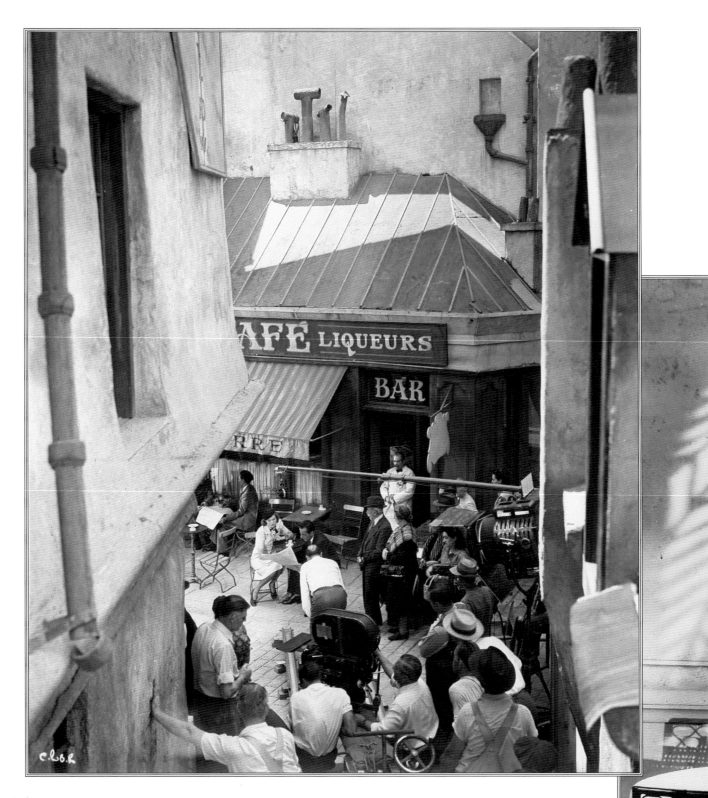

PREVIOUS OVERLEAF PAGES: Victor Laszlo (Paul Henreid) leads the orchestra at Rick's in "La Marseillaise," one of several scenes carried over from the play EVERYBODY COMES TO RICK'S. ABOVE: The Montmartre café where Rick and Ilsa discuss the German approach to Paris in one of the first scenes shot for the film.

LEFT: Art Director Carl Jules Weyl designed the entryway that turned the Los Angeles Airport into Casablanca. The tower (right) is an actual part of the airport and still stands today. BELOW: Part of the set for Rick's Café.

Of All The
GIN JOINTS
In All the Towns In All
THE WORLD,
She Walks Into Mine

BELOW: Sign marking the entrance to Warner Bros. At the time EVERYBODY COMES TO RICK'S arrived there, the studio was home to such stars as Humphrey Bogart, George Brent, James Cagney, Bette Davis, Olivia de Havilland, Geraldine Fitzgerald, John Garfield, Ida Lupino, Ronald Reagan, Edward G. Robinson, and Ann Sheridan.
BOTTOM: Hal Wallis's memo changing the film's title from EVERYBODY COMES TO RICKS'S to CASABLANCA.

On December 8, 1941, the day after the Japanese attack on Pearl Harbor, the script that would become *Casablanca* walked into—or, rather, was delivered to—the office of studio reader Stephen Karnot. Like most such readers, Karnot was responsible for evaluating manuscripts in terms of their cinematic potential. Within three days, he had finished *Everybody Comes to Rick's*. The report he sent to Warner Bros. producer Hal Wallis consisted of a one-page synopsis, a twenty-two-page synopsis, and the following brief comments:

Excellent melodrama. Colorful, timely background, tense mood, suspense, psychological and physical conflict, tight plotting, sophisticated hokum. A box-office natural—for Bogart, or Cagney, or Raft in out-of-the-usual roles and perhaps Mary Astor.

By December 22, Wallis had read the report and decided he wanted to make this movie. *Everybody Comes to Rick's* was on its way to becoming a part of film history.

Even before Warners purchased *Everybody Comes to Rick's*, Wallis was developing the project. In fact, the title was changed to *Casablanca* on New Year's Eve of 1941, and the first trade-paper announcement of the upcoming film appeared a week before the contracts were signed. On January 12, 1942, Warner Bros. paid $20,000, reportedly the highest fee ever paid for an unproduced play, to playwrights Murray Burnett and Joan Allison.

There were a variety of reasons for Wallis's enthusiasm for the property. With U.S. entry into the war against the Axis, Hollywood was scrambling for projects to support and capitalize on the war effort. *Everybody Comes to Rick's*, a tale of a U.S. expatriate involved with refugees struggling to escape to America, seemed like an ideal choice. In addition, the play's North African setting evoked memories of the 1938 hit, *Algiers*, in which Charles Boyer and Hedy Lamarr had shared a doomed love in that exotic city.

According to one of the many legends surrounding *Casablanca*'s creation, there is little similarity between the film and the unproduced play. In truth, the two have a great deal in common.

Like *Casablanca*, *Everybody Comes to Rick's* focuses on an American, Rick Blaine, running a café in the French Moroccan city of Casablanca. Blaine is hiding from a dark secret in his past, a lost love whose betrayal has turned him into an isolated loner. His cynical front is shattered when the woman shows up as the traveling companion of Victor Laszlo, a noted resistance fighter trying to get to the U.S.

A pair of powerful exit visas has been stolen by a black-market figure named Ugarte, who asks Rick to hold them. When Ugarte is arrested and, subsequently, commits suicide, Rick's Café becomes the center of intrigue as Laszlo and his companion, who realizes she still

WARNER BROS. FIRST NATIONAL
And COSMOPOLITAN PRODUCTIONS
BURBANK, CAL.
The World's Largest Motion Picture Studio
APRIL 5, 1937

With the exception of one scene, the world of CASABLANCA would be created here, in the Warner Bros. soundstages. The 135-acre facility in Burbank, acquired in a merger with First National in 1928, represented a major asset for the fast-rising studio and was considered one of the most modern film lots in Hollywood. Today, the lot is shared with Columbia Pictures and bears the official name "The Burbank Studios."

loves Rick; the local Vichy police captain, Luis Rinaldi; and the Nazi officer, Captain Strasser, all vie to get their hands on the visas. The situation is resolved when Rick pretends he is going to turn in Laszlo, but instead holds Rinaldi at gunpoint until the resistance leader can get on the plane to Lisbon. Rick also sends his true love off, arguing that she needs to keep fighting beside Victor. After they leave, Strasser arrives to lead Rick off to jail.

The major difference between *Everybody Comes to Rick's* and *Casablanca* is the character of Rick's lost love. The leading lady in the play is not Victor's saintly wife, Ilsa, but rather an American woman of easy virtue named Lois Meredith. She and Rick first met in Paris. For a year, they had a passionate affair, despite her knowledge that he was married and had two children. But when Rick discovered she was

being kept by another man, he was so shattered that he divorced his wife and ran off to Casablanca. At the time of her arrival in North Africa, Lois does not appear to have changed her ways. She is not married to Victor, and on her first night in the city, she sleeps with Rick to get her hands on the exit visas [see Appendix].

Such a plot development would not have been allowed in the Hollywood of the forties, when the studios operated under a strict code of self-censorship. To get advice on how to deal with this and other problems the play posed, Wallis solicited opinions from a variety of people on the lot, including writers Robert Lord, Aeneas McKenzie, Wally Kline, Robert Buckner, Casey Robinson, Jerry Wald, and Philip and Julius Epstein; and directors William Keighley, Vincent Sherman, and Michael Curtiz.

The responses were, for the most part,

Ever the life of the party, Jack L. Warner picks up the check as his wife Ann (left) and star Carole Landis (standing) look on.

encouraging. Wald thought it would be a great vehicle for George Raft or Humphrey Bogart and also suggested that the script be tailored along the lines of *Algiers*. McKenzie pointed out the appeal of the central theme, the need for faith in ideals, but like several others who read the script, he expressed concern about the censorable relationship between Rick and Lois. Kline suggested that once the censorable material was removed there would be little script left.

The most negative response came from Buckner, who, besides complaining about censorship problems, labeled the play's big moment "sheer hokum." He also derided Rick's characterization as "two-parts Hemingway, one-part Scott Fitzgerald, and a dash of cafe Christ."

There are no memos on record from Robinson, Sherman, the Epsteins, or Curtiz, who all appear to have delivered favorable judgments to Wallis in person. Robinson, the writer of *Captain Blood* and *Dark Victory*, has claimed to have read the script first, during a railroad trip with Wallis, recommending it to the producer the next day. Robinson has also stated that he hoped either to make the script his first independent production or, at the very least, to write the film for his friend. Wallis's decision to go ahead and produce the film himself was a great disappointment to Robinson.

In an oral history on file at the American Film Institute, Vincent Sherman, too, claims to have recommended the script to Wallis. Robert Rossen, later the writer-director of *Body and Soul* and *The Hustler*, came into Sherman's office one morning in January 1942 and mentioned a "piece of crap that is being sent around called *Everybody Comes to Rick's*." After lunch, Sherman received his own copy, along with a note asking for his opinion of it. Unlike Rossen, Sherman saw a lot of cin-

On Tour with "Dantes Inferno"- the first Picture Road Show. Atlantic City 1910.

Jack (far right) and Sam Warner (second from right) in front of an Atlantic City theater in which they had booked the Italian silent film DANTE'S INFERNO in 1910. In an early distribution deal, the two took the epic to theaters in Connecticut and New Jersey, scoring a $1,500 profit that they lost shortly thereafter in a crap game.

ematic potential in it. "It [had] all of the things that used to make me go to pictures as a kid," he would say years later. "Strange and interesting backgrounds. Strange and interesting people from all of the countries of the world. Strange and interesting doings going on."

He immediately told the Epsteins to be on the lookout for the material and got them worked up about it. At the end of the day, Sherman caught Wallis just as the producer was leaving his office. Wallis was pleased to hear of the Epsteins' interest in the project, but he turned down Sherman's offer to help them work up a script on the grounds that the director was already too busy with plans for *The Hard Way*.

Wallis's next job was to assign the script to a writer. After considering Lenore Coffee and radio writer Arch Oboler, both of whom were heavily involved with other scripts at the time, Wallis chose Aeneas McKenzie and Wally Kline. In his autobiography, *Starmaker*, Wallis states that he chose McKenzie because of the writer's facility with European characters and settings, as demonstrated in his script for *Juarez*.

The day after receiving the assignment, McKenzie applied to the Warner Bros. Research Department for photographs of Casablanca. As was the case at the other major studios, the research department at Warner Bros. was responsible for supplying and checking virtually every piece of information related to the studio's productions. Through the course of preparations for *Casablanca*, Dr. Herman Lissauer's staff would provide McKenzie with lyrics to "As Time Goes By" and the *"Horst Wessel,"* send pictures of Moroccan and Tunisian women to costume designer Orry-Kelly, and prepare a virtual bible on North

If It's December 1941 In Casablanca, What Time Is It In New York?

espite the fact that World War II had started on September 1, 1939, by December 1941, the time at which *Casablanca* is set, most Americans persisted in their belief that the U.S. could—and indeed *should*—stay out of that "phony war in Europe." In fact, a Gallup poll held during the early years of the war indicated that 96 percent of all Americans wanted the country to remain neutral.

But at Warners, good headlines made good movies: in 1938, four Nazi agents were convicted of espionage in a case recounted in "Storm Over America," a series of *New York Post* articles by former FBI man Leon G. Turrou. J. Edgar Hoover suggested that a film version of those articles could help awaken Americans to the Nazi threat, and Jack Warner agreed. The result was *Confessions of a Nazi Spy*, a 1939 film with one-time gangster star Edward G. Robinson as an FBI man, Frances Lederer as a Nazi agent who ends up as an informant, and Paul Lukas and George Sanders as the heads of the spy ring. To guarantee the film's authenticity, Hal Wallis arranged for screenwriter Morton Krims to go undercover to German-American Bund meetings.

The film garnered strong praise, with critic and documentarian Pare Lorentz writing, "The Warner brothers have declared war on Germany with this one....Everybody duck." At year's end, it even won the National Board of Review's Best Picture award over such minor contenders as *Gone With the Wind*, *Mr. Smith Goes to Washington*, *Stagecoach*, and *Wuthering Heights*.

Another 1939 feature dealt indirectly

Philip Dorn (center) as the German resistance fighter in Warners' topical melodrama UNDERGROUND. The role made him one of two leading contenders to play Victor Laszlo in CASABLANCA. The other was Paul Henreid.

with events in Europe. *Juarez*, with Paul Muni as the Abraham Lincoln of Mexico, portrayed people rising up against the Hapsburg emperor set up by France's Napoleon III, a plot with strong parallels to the Nazi occupation of Czechoslovakia.

If nineteenth-century Mexico could supply a parallel to war-torn Europe, then why not Elizabethan England? With swashbuckling Errol Flynn drawing crowds, Warners remade *The Sea Hawk*. Flynn played a role modeled on Sir Francis Drake, who preyed on Spanish ships in the days just before the attempted invasion of England in 1588. Writer Howard Koch, one of the three men credited for *Casablanca*'s screenplay, seized the opportunity to write a stirring speech for Queen Elizabeth in defiance of Spanish imperialism. Few in 1940 could fail to relate it to the British position under German air attack.

Warners' next major war film was set during World War I, and the message was even stronger. As written by Howard Koch and John Huston and directed by Howard Hawks, *Sergeant York* was designed to show Americans what they would be fighting for in the years to come. It became the top-grossing film of its year and brought Gary Cooper the Oscar and New York Film Critics Award for Best Actor.

At other studios, Charles Chaplin triggered a furor by daring to make light of the Third Reich in *The Great Dictator*. Walter Wanger's *Foreign Correspondent*, directed by Alfred Hitchcock, had a fanciful plot about the Nazis kidnapping of a Dutch diplomat, but no overt mention of the Germans. At MGM, Norma Shearer helped Robert Taylor

CONFESSIONS OF A NAZI SPY may have "opened the eyes of 130,000,000 Americans," but it also triggered bomb threats, the burning of a Milwaukee theater, and an outcry from conservative politicians. As a result, Warners set its political commentary in other time periods, including World War I, which served as the backdrop for 1941's biggest box-office hit, SERGEANT YORK (shown in production, below), with Gary Cooper (top right) in the title role.

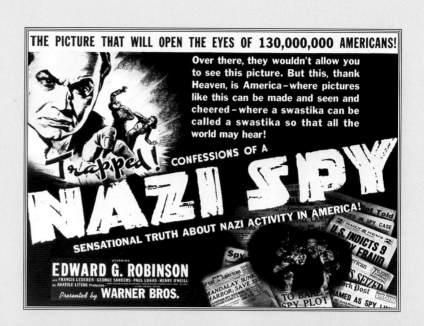

get his mother out of a concentration camp in *Escape* without ever using the words "German" or "Nazi."

In 1941, Warners released *Underground*. The film depicted the conflict between two brothers, resistance fighter Philip Dorn and loyal Nazi Jeffrey Lynn, reflecting events in the headlines. In fact, the script was updated during filming to incorporate news reports from the European front.

There was some strong opposition to such features. One of the government's leading isolationists, Senator Gerald P. Nye, pushed for a senate hearing at which Jack L. Warner and other studio heads heard charges that they were producing pro-war propaganda, partly to prevent the loss of income from British theaters. But the hearings would be abandoned when the U.S. entered the war a few months later.

By November 1942, when *Casablanca* premiered in New York, America had been at war for almost a year, a situation reflected in one way or another by almost every U.S. film. In fact, poverty-row studio Republic Pictures released *Remember Pearl Harbor*, Hollywood's first true World War II film, just four months after the actual attack.

As quickly as possible, filmmakers like John Ford, John Huston, Frank Capra, William Wyler, and five hundred other industry members finished their entertainment pictures and got to work making films for the government. At Warner Bros., talent made available to the War Department included, most notably, writers Julius J. and Philip G. Epstein, who took a break from writing *Casablanca* to join Frank Capra in Washington and create a series of seven films under the umbrella title *Why We Fight*. Warners also produced some six hundred training and propaganda films under the supervision of Owen Crump of the studio's shorts department.

In return for such cooperation, the government granted Hollywood a number of valu-

In THE SEA HAWK, Flora Robson (left), as Elizabeth I, seems to be addressing contemporary audiences as she speaks to the kneeling Errol Flynn: "...when the ruthless ambitions of a man threaten to engulf the world it becomes the solemn obligation of free men...to affirm that the earth belongs...to all men and that freedom is the deed and title to the soil on which we exist."

able concessions. The Selective Service System declared filmmaking an "essential industry," thus placing strong price controls on equipment and materials and freeing the studios' staffs, including actors, from the draft. The Justice Department stopped pursuing its antitrust cases against studios that owned theater chains. And with the war-related loss of European revenues, the Office of the Coordinator of Inter-American Affairs helped the film industry develop markets in South and Central America, which accounts for the plethora of Latin American settings, subjects, and musical performers in films of this period.

From 1942 to 1945, Hollywood released

One of the many ways in which Hollywood aided the war effort was through celebrity appearances at bond drives. Here Judy Garland (standing left) and Mickey Rooney (seated to her right) are among the superstars selling democracy to an adoring public.

1,700 features, 500 of which dealt directly with war subjects. The government outlined six basic feature-film themes that would do the most to help the country: 1) pictures dealing with war issues and the American way of life; 2) pictures depicting the enemy and enemy philosophy; 3) pictures reflecting well on our allies; 4) pictures showing the industrial effort at home; 5) pictures showing what people could do on the homefront to support the war effort; and 6) pictures showing our fighting forces at work.

As intended, the films produced under these guidelines provided popular entertainment and solidified the nation's support for the war effort and the Allies.

African life for Michael Curtiz.

McKenzie and Kline submitted their final script pages on February 23, at which point their work was done. That the first writers assigned to *Casablanca* were taken off the film so soon does not in any way reflect on their work. Although Warners had always tried to minimize rewrites and the number of writers assigned to each film, the other Hollywood majors frequently used a writer or writing team to do an initial draft from which someone else would prepare the final shooting script. In the case of *Casablanca*, McKenzie and Kline may have been expected to do no more than a rough adaptation of *Everybody Comes to Rick's*, simply translating the property from its stage origins to a more cinematic form and cleaning up basic censorship problems.

Beyond the patriotic message, the cover art for this issue of the **Warner Bros.** in-house employee newsletter demonstrates the way in which Hollywood caricatured the enemy. Images like these would return to haunt their creators in more recent years, making some of the studio's wartime product virtually unscreenable today.

The script then went to twin brothers Julius J. and Philip G. Epstein, who had had the best possible training for work in Hollywood—as schoolboys they cleaned their father's livery stable on a daily basis. Julius fell in love with writing while attending Penn State and developed a special interest in the comic classics of Richard Brinsley Sheridan, William Congreve, and Molière. But on graduation, he found little market for an untried writer.

So, he turned to work as a publicist, promoting the conductor of radio's "The Kate Smith Hour." Churning out press releases helped him polish his writing skills, particularly the razor-sharp wit that would become the Epsteins' trademark. It also put Julius into contact with two newspapermen who were on the road to Hollywood, Mark Hellinger and Jerry Wald.

Wald went to Hollywood in the early thirties and won a writing assignment at Warner Bros. Feeling he was not good enough to do the screenplay, he wired Epstein in New York and offered him $25 a week to ghost the script. Epstein agreed, and in no time completed *Twenty Million Sweethearts*, a vehicle for Dick Powell and Ginger Rogers.

Over the next eighteen months, when not writing screenplays for Wald, Epstein churned out ideas for film stories. When he finally sold one, Epstein generously agreed to share the credit with Wald. The result was *Living on Velvet*—a 1935 society drama starring Kay Francis and Warren William—and a Warner Bros. contract.

Epstein did well at Warners. He teamed with Lenore Coffee in 1938 to write a film for the Lane Sisters (Rosemary, Lola, and Priscilla), *Four Daughters*, a box-office smash combining family drama, social commentary, and classical music. The picture introduced John Garfield to film audiences and brought Julius his first Oscar nomination.

By this time, Julius had already collaborated with his brother on a stage play, *And Stars Remain*, which had some success when produced in New York by the Theatre Guild. Philip also had written a few pictures of his own, including the screwball comedy *The Mad Miss Manton*, starring Barbara Stanwyck and Henry Fonda, which put him in a position to get a contract at Warner Bros.

The twins became one of the studio's most reliable writing teams. They helped turn S. N. Berhman's sophisticated stage play *No Time for Comedy* into a screen hit starring Rosalind Russell and James Stewart, and followed that with *The Bride Came C.O.D.*, a rare comic vehicle for Bette Davis, and two more stage adaptations, *The Man Who Came to Dinner* and *The Male Animal*.

When the Epsteins took over writing *Casablanca*, time was of the essence. Wallis had already set his sights on Humphrey Bogart for the male lead, so shooting would have to be scheduled for late spring or early summer, before Bogie went to Columbia Pictures on a loan-out agreement. The Epsteins had made arrangements to fly to Washington, D.C., to help director Frank Capra with his *Why We Fight* documentary series. Although they would be off salary during their month or so in the capital, they would work on the *Casablanca* script in their spare time and be paid only if it proved acceptable.

The Epsteins worked on *Casablanca* in Washington, roughly from February 25 to March 16, 1942. At some time during that period, they sent their first pages to Wallis. This draft of the first third of the script—running through the start of the Paris flashback—is dated April 2, 1942.

This script clearly points the way to the final film, but maintains many similarities to the play. The female lead is still the American Lois Meredith, a vain, morally questionable character. When she is informed of Ugarte's arrest, her response is, "I imagine his cell is

Behind-the-scenes shot taken during the filming of THIS IS THE ARMY. The flag-waving 1943 musical fit the public mood perfectly, becoming the top-grossing picture of its year.

more comfortable than our suite at the hotel." The scene in which she and Rick reminisce about their parting in Paris introduces one of *Casablanca*'s most famous lines, but with a spin that emphasizes her shallowness:

> RICK: I remember every detail. The Germans wore gray, you wore blue.
> LOIS: Yes, I put that dress away. When the Germans march out I'll wear it again.
> RICK: That style should be back by then.

The Epsteins altered the character of Rinaldo, changing his name to Louis Renault (later they claimed they had named him after the car). The team envisioned the role being played by one of their favorite actors, Claude

The House That Jack, Harry, Sam, and Albert Built

The magic that turned *Everybody Comes to Rick's* into *Casablanca* was Hollywood's stock in trade. The major studios—Columbia, Paramount, MGM, RKO, 20th Century–Fox, United Artists, Universal, and Warner Bros.—ran like factories, producing escapist dreams on a regular basis to fill the voracious appetites of the large film-going public. The keystone of this arrangement was the seven-year contract, whereby talent in a variety of areas was tied to the fortunes of a single studio.

Because of these contracts, each studio developed a personal look or house style. Among the most distinctive were MGM, with its glossy dramas, comedies, and musicals, all emphasizing glamour and simple family values; Paramount, which provided exotic, sophisticated romances in the thirties before shifting to more down-home entertainment after a change in management in the forties; and Warner Bros., where playing it hard and fast was the rule of thumb.

Jack, Harry, Sam, and Albert Warner

The brothers Warner—(left to right) Sam, Harry, Jack, and Albert—rose from nickelodeon management to film distribution to production, eventually creating one of Hollywood's major studios. Sam died in 1927, leaving control of the studio in Jack and Harry's hands.

were the children of Jewish immigrants who had come to the U.S. from Poland in 1883. After much moving around, the family settled in Youngstown, Ohio, where the Warner brothers opened a nickelodeon in 1904. Movies did well for the Warners. After creating their own touring motion-picture show, they entered distribution. By 1918, they had acquired the film rights to *My Four Years in Germany*, ex-Ambassador James W. Gerard's memoirs recounting Germany's preparations for World War I. Combining documentary footage with scenes shot in New York, the brothers produced their first hit.

The following year, they opened a small studio on Sunset Boulevard in Hollywood, producing two or three pictures a year. As their films continued to show profits, the brothers Warner decided to incorporate as Warner Bros. in 1923. They also expanded their operations, acquiring the services of a young writer named Darryl F. Zanuck, a publicity assistant named Hal Wallis, and a well-trained canine named Rin Tin Tin.

Before long Warners entered a partnership with Western Electric to create the Vitaphone Company, which led to the film that ushered in the sound era, *The Jazz Singer*. As audiences lined up for that part-talkie in 1927, Warners and the rest of Hollywood moved full-speed-ahead into sound-film production. In July 1928, Warners released the first full talkie, *Lights of New York*, followed two months later by Jolson's follow-up to *The Jazz Singer*. *The Singing Fool* was the biggest hit in the studio's history.

Warners continued to expand, buying the Stanley Corporation of America, one of the nation's largest theater chains, in 1928, and the First National company, whose Burbank studios would become the new Warner Bros. headquarters, in 1929. Sadly, Sam Warner died of pneumonia the day before *The Jazz Singer* premiered. That left Warners in the hands of President Harry Warner, who ran the New York office, and Jack Warner, who headed the studios in Hollywood, with Albert as company treasurer.

By this time, Darryl F. Zanuck had risen to the position of production chief, developing the house style that would prevail through the thirties. Faced with sudden business reversals and falling attendance during the early days of the Great Depression, Zanuck produced a series of fast-paced, quickly shot films that combined the virtues of low cost with a topicality and energy that kept audiences coming back for more.

In 1933, Warners joined the rest of the industry in cutting back salaries to help the studios weather the Depression. At the end of eight weeks, the Motion Picture Academy declared that salaries could be restored. But Harry Warner decided not to restore them. An outraged Zanuck quit, eventually going on to create the independent 20th Century Pictures, which would merge with Fox in 1935.

Meanwhile, Hal Wallis carried on the house style Zanuck had created. By the mid-thirties, Warners was thriving once more, as was the rest of Hollywood. The studio began moving into more expensive productions, particularly after the success of the Errol Flynn–Olivia de Havilland swashbuckler *Captain Blood* in 1935 and the Paul Muni historical drama *The Story of Louis Pasteur* in 1936. The studio also produced a series of highly succesful romances starring Bette Davis—including *Jezebel*, *Dark Victory*, and *The Old Maid*—along with vehicles for such popular stars as James Cagney and Edward G. Robinson.

This was the world into which *Casablanca*, or rather *Everybody Comes to Rick's*, would arrive in December 1941.

Rains, and gave Renault more and more witty lines, the type of material they knew Rains could play to perfection. In this draft, Rains meets Strasser at the airport and assures him that everything is being done to find the killer of the two German couriers: "Realizing the importance of the case, my men are rounding up twice the usual number of suspects." Later, when Rick proposes a 5,000-franc wager on whether or not Laszlo will get out of Casablanca, Renault asks for a smaller bet on the grounds that "I am only a poor corrupt official." He would be even poorer by the time the line reached the screen. In later drafts the 5,000-franc bet, worth $114.15 in the early 1940s, was doubled.

Rick, too, is given his share of humorous lines, as in his famous evasion of Renault's questions about his past:

RENAULT: ...what in heaven's name brought you to Casablanca?
RICK: My health. I came to Casablanca for the waters.
RENAULT: Waters? What waters? We're in the desert.
RICK: I was misinformed.

And when Strasser asks his opinion about the possibility of the Germans invading New York, Rick replies, "Well, there are certain sections of New York, Major, that I wouldn't advise you to try to invade." Nor is he the least bit disconcerted by Strasser's dossier on him, looking it over and replying simply, "Are my eyes really brown?"

What is missing in Rick's characterization is any reference to his past. Neither his marriage, nor the play's admittedly meager references to his political involvement are present. Julius Epstein later said that he and his brother deliberately skipped over that part of his background, with every intention of returning to the script later to flesh things out. What they devised, however, was the perfect expression of Rick's detachment: "I stick my neck out for nobody."

ABOVE: Julius J. (left) and Philip G. Epstein became Warner's top writing team because of their wit and sense of structure, qualities that helped make CASABLANCA a crowd pleaser. BELOW: One of history's least heralded playwriting teams was born when aspiring actress Joan Allison (left, with unidentified man) met writer Murray Burnett.

Victor Laszlo is much as he was in the original script, though this draft drops the references to his fortune. Instead of money, Strasser's goal is to get the names of Laszlo's fellow resistance workers. A new scene, between Victor and a member of the resistance named Berger, clearly demonstrates the character's importance to the underground movement.

Structurally, the Epstein draft is very similar to the finished film. The script opens with a spinning globe and a voice-over explaining the refugee trail. The nature of life in Casablanca is set up with several short scenes, including the police's shooting of a civilian with no identification papers and the antics of a pickpocket labeled "The Dark European."

The Epsteins retained the scenes Burnett and Allison used to set up Rick's character—the exchanges with Ugarte, Rick's refusal to drink with the customers, and the argument with the Englishman who has been denied access to the gambling room. But they added an important scene in which Carl, the headwaiter, informs Rick that one of the patrons at the roulette table is a compulsive gambler who has been trying for months to raise the money for an exit visa but keeps betting his savings away. Rick advises the player to bet on a particular number, which comes up repeatedly until the man has enough money to leave. This, of course, would become the resolution of the Jan and Annina subplot.

With these sixty-six pages of script, the Epsteins helped *Everybody Comes to Rick's* take a giant step towards becoming *Casablanca*.

Colonel Jack Warner

When Jack Warner was asked to make films for the Army Air Corps, he also was offered a commission, a title designed as much as a sign of gratitude as a badge of authority. Initially, he asked to be made a general, partly because his former second-in-command, Darryl F. Zanuck, had already been commissioned as a full colonel. The title lieutenant colonel was a step down from his expectations, but that did not keep him from wearing it with pride.

His first step was to order a uniform from the Warner Bros. Wardrobe Department (billed to the budget of one of the films in production, of course). He boned up on military protocol and, for the duration, signed all correspondence Col. Warner and insisted that his staff salute him.

Half-a-century later, thirteen years after Warner's death, his military pretensions would provide filmmakers Joel and Ethan Coen with one of the biggest laughs in their eccentric Hollywood black comedy *Barton Fink*. As head of the fictional Capitol Pictures, Michael Lerner wears a colonel's uniform to fire the title character played by John Turturro.

Like several other movie moguls, Jack Warner was offered an honorary commission in return for his studio's cooperation with the war effort. Unlike the other studio heads, however, Warner took his new title literally, going to work in uniform and insisting that his staff address him as "Col. Warner."

CEUX DE LA LEGIO

CELUI-LA EST ALLEMAND. LA MOITIE DU RECRUTEMENT DE LA LEGION CONTINUE A ETRE ALLEMANDE. ILS SONT BLONDS, ROSES, RASES. CE SONT D'ADMIRABLES SOLDATS. ILS NE PROTESTENT JAMAIS CONTRE LA DISCIPLINE MAIS CE SONT CEUX QUI, LA NUIT, SOUS LA TENTE, PLEURENT LE PLUS SOUVENT.

IL EST POLONAIS, IL SERT LA LEGION DEPUIS VINGT-CINQ ANS. IL A ETE BLESSE LE 28 FEVRIER 1933, A L'ATTAQUE DU DJEBEL SAGHO, A COTE DU LEGENDAIRE CAPITAINE BOURNAZEL, QUI FUT TUE PAR LA MEME RAFALE DE BALLES. DANS HUIT JOURS, ON LE LIBERERA ET IL REPARTIRA VERS LA VIE.

VOICI UN DES CLASSIQUES TATOUES. LA PLUPART DES HOMMES LE SONT A LA LEGION, SOIT PAR BRAVADE OU A LA SUITE D'UN PARI. MAIS C'EST LA UNE COUTUME PRESQUE EXCLUSIVEMENT RESER-VEE AUX SOLDATS FRANÇAIS. A LA LEGION, EN EFFET, LES ETRANGERS NE SE FONT PAS TATOUER.

CET HOMME SERT SOUS LE DRAPEAU DE LA LEGION DEPUIS TRENTE ET UN ANS. LIBERE AU BOUT DE VINGT-CINQ ANS, IL S'EST RENGAGE SOUS UN AUTRE NOM. ON A FEINT DE NE PAS LE RECONNAITRE. IL A COMBATTU AUX QUATRE COINS DE L'EMPIRE FRANÇAIS. IL EST SOLDAT DE PREMIERE CLASSE.

44

IL A VINGT ANS. IL EST ESPAGNOL. IL N'A PAS SU CHOISIR ENTRE L'IDEAL DE FRANCO ET L'ID...
REPUBLICAINS. LA MOITIE DE SA FAMILLE COMBAT L'AUTRE MOITIE. SA MAISON A ETE BRULEE...
VENU A LA LEGION COMME ON VIENT AU COUVENT. IL NE VEUT PAS QU'ON LUI PARLE DE L'ES...

CE CAPITAINE EST UN ETRANGER D'UNE NOBLE FAMILLE GEORGIENNE. IL SERT A LA LEGION D...
VINGT ANS. DEPUIS QU'IL N'Y A PLUS DE COMBATS AU MAROC, IL DIRIGE LES COMPAGNIES DE...
...IERS QUI FONT DES PISTES A TRAVERS LE BLED. DANS UN MOIS, IL VA PARTIR POUR LE TO...

LES MERVEILLES DE L'AUTRE FRANCE

MEKNÈS : LE SOUK DES FABRI-
CANTS JUIFS D'OBJETS EN FER-
BLANC.   PHOTO LÉVY ET NEURDEIN RÉUNIS.

MEKNÈS : MARCHAND
DE TAPIS A HAUTE
LAINE.   M. SATGE.

MEKNÈS : MARCHANDS DE PAIN,
SUR LA PLACE, A LA TOMBÉE DU
JOUR.   PHOTO LÉVY ET NEURDEIN RÉUNIS.

This is the Chamber of Commerce building in Casablanca, and it is a
splendid example of how the French are preserving the Moorish atmosphere by adhering to Moorish lines in all the modern buildings.

CASABLANCA background for
the film's writers, design-
ers, and director from
Warner Bros. Research
Department. French Foreign
Legion uniforms (left), "The
Marvels of the Other France"
(top), the Casablanca
Chamber of Commerce
(middle), and "The Nomadic
Tent" (bottom).

Chapter Two

ROUND UP

The Usual

SUSPECTS

The first official word about *Casablanca*'s casting was an announcement in *The Hollywood Reporter* for January 5, 1942. Two days later, the story was repeated in a press release headlined "SHERIDAN, REAGAN AND MORGAN TO BE STARRED IN *CASABLANCA*." The brief announcement read:

Ann Sheridan and Ronald Reagan will be teamed by Warner Bros. for the third time in *Casablanca*, a story about war refugees in French Morocco. They first played opposite each other in *Kings Row*, not yet released, and then were teamed again in *Juke Girl*, recently completed.

Dennis Morgan will be the third member of a starring trio in *Casablanca*. The film is to be based on *Everybody Comes to Rick's*, an unproduced play written by Murray Burnett and Joan Allison.

This announcement has been a source of bewilderment to the film's fans and historians for decades. By what stretch of the imagination would anyone consider casting Ronald Reagan as Rick? The callow young actor in such films as *Dark Victory* and *Kings Row* was hardly the type to be cast as a grizzled, cynical anti-hero. The total implausibility of such casting gives credibility to the legend that *Casablanca* was originally intended as a B film.

But it wasn't. Hal Wallis was far from a B-film producer, and Reagan, Sheridan, and Morgan were all being given star buildups. Reagan had impressed fans with his work as the young George Armstrong Custer in *Santa Fe Trail* and had a plum role in *Kings Row*. Sheridan was also in the latter prestige production and had scored a personal triumph in *Torrid Zone*, which built on her image as "The Oomph Girl." And Morgan had a hit of his own as the weak-willed blue blood in love with Ginger Rogers in *Kitty Foyle*.

Actually, there is nothing in the announcement to indicate which actor was to play which role. Given the weight of their screen images at the time, it is altogether possible, as some historians have suggested, that Reagan was meant to play Victor and Morgan to play Rick—if they were ever seriously intended for the roles at all.

Reagan has stated that he was never approached about playing either role. The only other mention of Reagan and Morgan was in connection with finding someone to test with one of the actresses being considered for the female lead, but contract players between assignments were expected to perform in tests, even when they were not involved in the film in question.

One explanation for the notice in the *Reporter* is simple. Wallis may have been in a hurry to stake a claim on the title *Casablanca*, a title he had chosen to underline the picture's similarity to *Algiers*. With no stars firmly in place, he or someone in the publicity department may

The first team of CASABLANCA all-stars as announced in "The Hollywood Reporter": (opposite) future president Ronald Reagan; (below) 'Oomph Girl' Ann Sheridan and Irish tenor Dennis Morgan.

have decided to use the announcement to keep the names of some of the studio's more promising younger players in the press.

Wallis knew who he wanted as the male lead, however. *Casablanca* was the perfect vehicle to make Humphrey Bogart a major star.

Humphrey DeForest Bogart was born in 1899 to money, not the New York 400, but money nonetheless. His father, Dr. Belmont DeForest Bogart, was one of New York's finest internists, while his mother, Maud Humphrey, was a noted portrait artist. In fact, Bogart's first professional "appearance" occurred when his mother sold a portrait of him to a baby-food company for use in their advertising. (Contrary to legend, however, it was not the Gerber Company, and Bogie was not the first Gerber Baby.)

At his father's urging, Bogart enrolled in the Phillips Academy in Andover, Massachusetts, in preparation for Yale Medical School, but the young man did not care for studying and eventually left Phillips. He enlisted in the Navy during World War I. Although he did not see much action, his Navy service would contribute an important element to his legend. During this period he acquired the scar that would give him his characteristic sneer and lisp.

There are at least three versions of how he got the scar. According to one story, it was caused by a piece of shrapnel that cut his lip during maneuvers on board the USS *Leviathan*, even though World War I had ended sixteen days before Bogie was assigned to the ship. Bogart-biographer Nathaniel Benchley's version of the story has Bogart being attacked by a military prisoner he was escorting to naval prison. Another tale occurs in Louise Brooks's fanciful, if highly perceptive, *Lulu in Hollywood*. According to her, Bogart had such a beautiful mouth—"very full, rosy, and perfectly modeled"—that he was considered almost effeminately attractive. Following one barroom brawl in which his lip was cut open,

he decided not to have it sewn up, just to give himself a tougher demeanor.

However it occurred, in 1919 Bogart emerged from the Navy with his trademark scar. Through a friend, he got a job in a Broadway production office and then worked as a stage manager. He soon turned to acting, because he thought it was an easy way to make money.

His first important role came in a 1922 melodrama titled *Swifty*. He played a callow young aristocrat who deflowered the leading lady before the curtain rose and dogged her steps until the end. The play was not received well, and Alexander Woollcott said Bogart's performance was "what is usually and mercifully described as inadequate," which would always be the actor's favorite review.

After many more juvenile roles and bad reviews, Bogart learned how to play within his callow, young, sophisticated type, and when he opened opposite Mary Boland in *Cradle Snatchers* in 1925, he not only got good reviews, he had his first hit. In 1930, Bogart made his screen debut in the short "Broadway's Like That." Most of his early films were forgettable. With little of interest on screen, he kept returning to Broadway. In 1934, director Arthur Hopkins called Bogie to audition for a new play by Robert E. Sherwood, then shocked both actor and writer by asking him to read for the part of an escaped murderer, Duke Mantee. The play was *The Petrified Forest*.

More important than the good notices he received—and he certainly got those—was the fact that Hopkins and leading man Leslie Howard exposed Bogart to a new school of acting. Previously, Bogart had gone through the motions, using the stilted, somewhat declamatory, self-centered style that most people thought of as "acting" at the time. But Hopkins and Howard took a subtler approach. Their goal was to capture reality as fully as possible through a simple, natural delivery and the creation of a seamless ensemble.

As almost all good plays do, *The Petrified Forest* made the journey to Hollywood. The

Raymond Guion 1926

In Hollywood the young Bogart (above) displayed the polished good looks that made him one of the stage's leading male ingenues. The juvenile Bogie (far right) had his greatest Broadway success in CRADLE SNATCHERS—co-starring (left to right) Gene Raymond, Raymond Hackett, and Mary Boland—in 1925. Boland, one of Broadway's most popular comediennes, had banned Bogart from her productions two years earlier after he forgot his last entrance in MEET THE WIFE and left the rest of the cast to improvise. After trying almost every other actor in town for the leading male role in CRADLE SNATCHERS, Boland finally agreed to work with him again.

Raymond
Hackett
1926

Mary Boland
1926
for
Cradle Snatchers

Humphrey
Bogart
1926

notably as the district attorney who gets nightclub hostess Bette Davis to turn state's evidence on her boss in *Marked Woman* and, on loan-out to Samuel Goldwyn, as the gangster returning to his Hell's Kitchen roots in *Dead End*—but, mostly, he was Cagney's or Robinson's less sympathetic colleague who got shot before the final fade-out.

He tried to better his lot by playing the press for all they were worth, building his reputation for combativeness, but that only alienated the studio management. And he didn't always stay true to form. He was so intimidated by the Dead End Kids during the filming of *Angels With Dirty Faces* that the young rowdies even got away with tearing off his pants during a break in filming.

In 1937, during the shooting of *Marked Woman*, he met a fiery supporting player named Mayo Methot, who was cast as one of Bette Davis's fellow hostesses. Though hardly a great actress, Methot was a woman of rare passion and volubility. Their affair brought out something in Bogart that few in Hollywood had seen previously. It also brought an end to his second marriage, to stage actress Mary Philips. (He had been briefly married to another actress, Helen Mencken, in the late twenties). Despite their passionate involvement, Bogart was in no hurry to marry Methot, but he finally gave in in 1938.

Bogart's career remained in the same rut for a while longer, reaching a low point in 1939, when he played a Mexican bandit in *The Oklahoma Kid* and a mute vampire in *The Return of Dr. X*. But he also landed an out-of-character supporting role as Bette Davis's horse-trainer in *Dark Victory*. The part wasn't much—half Blarney Stone, half D.H. Lawrence—but even with a bad brogue, he was

play was bought by Jack Warner, who wanted it for Edward G. Robinson. But Warner also wanted Leslie Howard to repeat his stage performance. When Howard learned his co-star and, by now, friend had been passed over, he promptly notified Warner that he would only do the film with Bogart as Duke Mantee. Bogie not only won the role, but a long-term contract as well, even though with Robinson and James Cagney already under contract for tough-guy leads, Warners did not have a lot for Bogart to do. He had a few good roles—most

George Raft would have played Rick if he had had any say in the matter. Like Bogart, Raft had his first screen successes in gangster roles; he even had some off-screen mob connections of his own. Late in his career, Raft got to play Rick Blaine in real life when he opened a gambling casino.

more interesting than the other major supporting male in the picture, Ronald Reagan.

It is hard to tell exactly why the studio suddenly decided to give him a star buildup. Possibly Warners needed insurance in the face of continuing rebellion from James Cagney and Edward G. Robinson. Also, Bogart's supporters on the lot, most notably writer John Huston and director Raoul Walsh, were gaining in prestige and were in a good position to push for him to get better roles.

In 1940, Huston and W.R. Burnett wrote a great script about a gangster who leaves prison only to find that the criminal ways of the past are dying. His efforts to pull off one last big heist are thwarted by cowardly cohorts and his misplaced affection for a shallow country girl. In a stirring mountaintop

The role of Sam Spade in THE MALTESE FALCON came courtesy of Bogart's good friend John Huston, who wrote the adaptation of Dashiell Hammett's novel and made his directing debut with the film. The film's popularity helped the actor's rise to stardom. This was the third version of the classic detective tale. Ricardo Cortez played Spade in 1931's THE MALTESE FALCON. In 1936, Warren William took over the role (opposite Bette Davis) in SATAN MET A LADY.

finale, he is killed by the police in a hail of gunfire. Amazingly, this plot was fresh at the time, and even if it had not been, Huston and Burnett's treatment was top-notch. However, none of the studio's top stars could see its merits; Paul Muni, James Cagney, and George Raft all turned the script down.

That was just the break Bogart needed. He landed the lead in *High Sierra* and finally got to show what he could really do as an actor. Even though "Mad Dog" Earle was still a gangster, the role had a sensitivity that he exploited to its fullest. It also gave Bogie his first shot at playing a cynical romantic, a man facing the realization that his dreams have not served him as well as they should have.

High Sierra brought Bogart his best reviews since *The Petrified Forest*, and because

of its box-office success, John Huston got the chance to direct his own adaptation of *The Maltese Falcon*. He wanted to cast Bogart as Sam Spade, but the studio demanded he offer the role to George Raft. Raft turned it down, saying that as a remake with an untried director, *The Maltese Falcon* would not be an important enough picture for him.

As Sam Spade, Bogart got to trade witticisms with Sydney Greenstreet, beat up Peter Lorre, and romance Mary Astor, who was considered a hot number at the time because of her recent scandalous divorce case. The role added a new dimension to his screen persona. Spade was a man of honor on his own terms. He may not have functioned strictly within the law, but there were lines he would not cross. He was a man who could turn in the woman he loved because she had killed his partner and "played him for a sap."

These two films made Bogart a star by setting up a tension between cynicism and idealism that no other screen actor had ever embodied quite so fully. But there was one element missing that would turn the star into a legend—passion. And that would be supplied in abundance by his role in *Casablanca*.

Yet, Jack Warner needed some convinc-

Bogart began his long-term Warner Bros. contract by re-creating his stage role as Duke Mantee in THE PETRIFIED FOREST (right) in 1936. By the end of the decade, that promising beginning seemed to have fizzled out thanks to such absurd roles as the near-silent vampire in THE RETURN OF DR. X (opposite). The film that salvaged Bogie's career was HIGH SIERRA (above), which gave the first indication of his star potential.

Bogart's performance in Casablanca anchors a film whose supporting cast represents a variety of images and acting styles. (Above) Rick consults with the croupier played by Marcel Dalio. (Right) In contrast to Dalio's naturalistic approach was the vaudeville-style clowning of S. Z. Sakall as Carl, the headwaiter.

ABOVE: Audiences enjoyed the cat-and-mouse games played by Bogart and Sydney Greenstreet in CASABLANCA as much as they had in the actors' two previous pictures together, THE MALTESE FALCON and ACROSS THE PACIFIC.

BELOW: Although Bogie could hold his own with CASABLANCA's more experienced character actors, he had no problem giving focus to the less experienced Joy Page, who made her screen debut as Annina Brandel, a refugee desparate for exit visas for her husband and herself.

The King of Casablanca

Hal Wallis was a quiet, withdrawn man very different from the more extroverted Jack Warner. The one thing the two men shared was a passionate love of movie-making that led to a string of hits for the studio.

Of all the artists who helped create *Casablanca*, the one whose over-all influence was strongest was producer Hal Wallis. It was he who chose the property, assigned the writers, decided which of their contributions would be filmed, hired the director and cast, approved every aspect of the production, and even wrote the final line. For many producers in Hollywood during the thirties and forties, filmmaking was strictly a business. In the hands of men like Wallis, David O. Selznick, Samuel Goldwyn, Arthur Freed, and Walt Disney, it became high art.

Like most of the great movie moguls, Wallis was a self-made man. He was born in Chicago in 1899 and forced to leave school at the age of fourteen to help support his family. His first success came as a traveling salesman, hawking electrical heating systems in the Midwest. But when his mother fell ill and needed to move to a warmer, drier climate, Wallis took her to Los Angeles and began looking for another job.

He had always been interested in the movies, so he used his selling skills to sweet-talk the head of a theater chain into hiring him as manager of the Garrick, one of the city's most important movie houses. There, he came into contact with Jack and Sam Warner, who gave him a job in their publicity department in 1923. Three months later, he was running the department. Publicity was an ideal area for Wallis, who had a natural ability to sell his ideas. In addition, he could learn the mechanics of film production and hone his skills at judging audience tastes.

When Sam Warner died, Jack needed someone he could trust to help him run the lot and turned to Wallis. As a producer, Wallis helped create many of the movies that established Warners' reputation in the early thirties: *Little Caesar, I Am a Fugitive from a Chain Gang, Gold Diggers of 1933,* and *Footlight Parade.* These films made it clear that Wallis was one of the studio's best investments, and when Darryl F. Zanuck left in 1933, Wallis became production chief. Over the next seven years, he supervised 371 features, while studio profits rose almost 700 percent. He also helped build the careers of James Cagney, Bette Davis, Humphrey Bogart, Errol Flynn, and Olivia de Havilland.

Jack Warner still had final say on all projects, and Wallis had to fight for anything that did not fit the boss's ideas of what would make money. Warner also resented his second-in-command because of the prevailing opinion that Wallis was the real reason for Warners' success.

By 1941, the situation came to a head. It was time to renegotiate Wallis's contract, but the production chief had other plans for his future. He proposed a new deal that would allow him to produce his own films on the lot

Wallis (left) with two stars under contract to David O. Selznick, Ingrid Bergman and Joseph Cotten. The latter was briefly considered to play Victor, but Selznick's $25,000-per-picture asking price for Cotten's services kept Wallis from pursuing the deal further.

with Warners' financing. Much to Wallis's surprise, Jack Warner agreed. Under the terms of his contract, Wallis had first pick of all stories bought by the studio and all personnel not currently engaged in production. From these, he would produce four films a year (six during the first year because of projects he already had in development) over a four-year period. And most important, each film would be billed as "A Hal B. Wallis Production."

Wallis's initial picture was *Now, Voyager.* It would be followed by such hits as *Air Force, Watch on the Rhine,* and the screen version of an unproduced play about an American caught between Nazi agents and resistance fighters in the French African city of Casablanca.

ing because of several run-ins he had had with the hard-headed star. Years earlier, Warner had rejected the idea of using Bogie in leading roles because, in his opinion, the actor's famous lisp made him sound "like a fairy." Possibly in retaliation, Bogart had circulated rumors that the studio head was homosexual. When Wallis suggested Bogart for *Casablanca*, legend has it that Warner responded with, "Who the hell would ever want to kiss Bogart?" Less plausible is another legend, that Ingrid Bergman was present at the time and chimed in with an enthusiastic, "I would." Whatever may or may not have happened, however, Warner finally agreed to casting Bogart in the film.

One of the most frequently quoted legends about *Casablanca* is that the role of Rick only went to Bogart because George Raft turned it down. Wallis even repeats the story in his autobiography. Challenging this is the fact that, although almost every other casting decision is well documented, there is not a single record of Raft's being offered the role. There is, however, a memo from Warner to Wallis dated April 2 that asks:

> What do you think of using Raft in *Casablanca*?
>
> He knows we are going to make this and is starting a campaign for it.

Wallis's response the next day would indicate that Raft was never a serious contender for the role:

> I have thought over very carefully the matter of George Raft in *Casablanca*, and I have discussed this with Mike [Curtiz], and we both feel that he should not be in the picture. Bogart is ideal for it, and it is being written for him, and I think we should forget Raft for this property.

Ingrid Bergman (opposite) radiated health and uncomplicated virtue, an image that proved a perfect fit to the character of Ilsa Lund. That image would stay with her throughout the forties, as demonstrated by the 1945 "Motion Picture" cover (above).

Incidentally, he hasn't done a picture here since I was a little boy, and I don't think he should be able to put his fingers on just what he wants to do when he wants to do it.

The matter of casting the female lead was more complicated. In his autobiography, Wallis states that he always wanted Ingrid Bergman for the role. Studio memos do not bear this out, however. Of the three players mentioned in that first announcement about *Casablanca*, the only one under serious consideration was Ann Sheridan. In a memo dated February 7, 1942, Wallis asked that a test be scheduled for her. A week later, he advised casting director Steve Trilling to work out the details for putting Sheridan and Bogart into the film.

At the same time, however, there were discussions of taking the character in a different direction. Casey Robinson was courting the Russian ballerina Tamara Toumanova during the early days of *Casablanca*'s preparation, and he claims that this inspired him to suggest making the leading lady a European, so his future wife could play the role.

The idea fit the picture perfectly. Suddenly, Rick would become the weary, neutral American, disenchanted with any kind of involvement in life but drawn back into the game by someone who knew what it meant to see her homeland overrun. The same memo in which Wallis asked for Sheridan's test stated that Toumanova was scheduled to test. Within days after his decision to use Sheridan, Wallis was actively pursuing the European idea, a fact verified by an undated letter from the Epsteins sometime in February or March:

> While we handle the foreign situation here, you try to get a foreign girl for the part. An American girl with big tits will do.
>
> Love & kisses,
> Julie & Phil

The two top European contenders to star

in *Casablanca* were Hedy Lamarr and Ingrid Bergman, although neither was available. Hedy Lamarr—who had starred in *Algiers*, the film on which *Casablanca* was being modeled—was under contract to MGM. Louis B. Mayer considered her his personal discovery and wanted his studio to take the lion's share of the credit for making her a star (until, of course, her pictures bombed, and he lost interest). Wallis's other choice for the role, Ingrid Bergman, was also unavailable.

Bergman was born in Stockholm in 1915. Her father was an artist who opened a photographic shop to convince his fiancée's German parents that he was stable enough to marry her. After seven years, they gave in.

When Ingrid was three, her mother died; the girl's memories of her would be based entirely upon faded photographs and home movies taken by her father. Nine years later, she watched her father waste away from cancer, leaving her to be raised by the strict, religious aunt who had moved in when her mother died. Within months of Ingrid's father, however, the aunt died sud-

Although the Bergman look was decidedly more natural than most screen stars of the time, the contrast between this 1937 portrait taken in Sweden (opposite) and the still (below) from INTERMEZZO: A LOVE STORY, her first Hollywood picture, indicates that there was some Hollywood glamor at work, despite the pronouncements of Bogart, David O. Selznick, and scores of publicists.

denly, passing away in the child's arms.

Ingrid moved in with an aunt and uncle with five children. But the household had none of the artistic charm of her father's home. Though the family was reasonably well off, helped greatly by Ingrid's inheritances from her father and her aunt, she felt dispossessed. Years earlier, Ingrid's father had taken her to a performance at Sweden's Royal Dramatic Theatre, and the young girl had romantically proclaimed her wish to be an actress. The sudden change in her life transformed that ambition into an obsession.

Using part of her inheritance, Ingrid hired private tutors in acting and gymnastics. In August 1933, she was chosen from approximately seventy-five applicants for one of eight openings at the Royal Dramatic School. Ingrid performed well during her first year of acting school. Then, during her summer vacation, she was given a screen test at Svensk Filmindustri. The test's director, Gustav Molander, immediately saw her screen potential and helped her land the ingenue role in *The*

Count From the Monk's Bridge, a comedy being filmed at the studio. She was so effective, they offered her a contract, and she left the Royal Dramatic School, becoming only the second student ever to walk out on the esteemed training program. The first was Greta Garbo.

Bergman worked steadily at Svensk Filmindustri, gradually building a following of fans and a scrapbook of good reviews. For her sixth film, in 1936, she was cast opposite the Swedish cinema's leading matinee idol, Gösta Ekman, with her mentor Molander as director. The picture was the romantic story of a married concert violinist who falls in love with his innocent young accompanist only to have their tryst end in a family tragedy. The title was *Intermezzo*.

It took a year for *Intermezzo* to reach the U.S., but when it did, it proved to be the turning point in Bergman's career. Independent producer David O. Selznick was in the market for foreign films he could remake for American audiences and had instructed his New York story editor Kay Brown (the same woman who brought *Gone With the Wind* to Selznick) to be on the look-out for such properties. According to legend, the Swedish elevator operator at the building where Brown worked told her about the picture after its New York opening (Brown has denied this anecdote). She went to the film in search of a story, but instead discovered a star.

In Brown's report on *Intermezzo*, she raved about Bergman's star potential, if not the film itself. Selznick liked both and planned to cast the actress in an American version of the story.

But that was without reckoning with Bergman herself. The actress had married a dentist named Petter Lindstrom and was eight months pregnant when Selznick's London rep-

After the success of **INTERMEZZO**, good parts and good films were hard to come by for Bergman. She got the former, if not the latter, when she played Ivy, the sluttish barmaid, in MGM's adaptation of **DR. JEKYLL AND MR. HYDE**, starring Spencer Tracy.

resentative first contacted her. At the time, she stated that she could not think of working outside of Sweden until 1940 at the earliest.

Of course, that was too late for Selznick, who was already hard at work casting his film. Other blandishments were made, including a deal for Molander to direct the American version. But still, she wouldn't budge. Selznick offered her Leslie Howard as a leading man. She decided she might be available by fall of 1939.

At this point, Selznick sent Brown to Stockholm to negotiate directly with Bergman. Molander was out of the picture by now, so Brown tempted her with the suggestion that William Wyler, who already was building his reputation internationally, might direct. Finally, Bergman agreed. She signed to make one film, *Intermezzo*, but also gave Selznick the right to use her in two pictures a year over the next five years. In return, she had the right to make two foreign-language films a year for other producers, though with the increasing unrest in Europe, that clause would never be excercised.

In May 1939, Ingrid Bergman hit Hollywood like a breath of fresh air. Her simple makeup, complete with natural eyebrows and a minimum of blush and lipstick, was a major departure from the Hollywood standard (this was only two years after Jean Harlow's death, and peroxide and pencil-thin eyebrows were still the norm). According to Bergman's biographer, Laurence Leamer, one noted actress who met her remarked, "We have enough trouble getting jobs as it is. Do they have to import kitchen maids?"

Bergman has claimed that she had to fight Selznick's orders to use more makeup. He, on the other hand, took credit for popularizing her natural look. Either way, her fresh,

The elite corps of actresses to lose star-making roles to Ingrid Bergman. RIGHT: Hedy Lamarr was unable to make CASABLANCA and later turned down GASLIGHT and SARATOGA TRUNK. BELOW, left to right: At first, Vera Zorina seemed to have beaten Bergman for the coveted role of Maria in FOR WHOM THE BELL TOLLS, but she lost out to her in the long run. Ann Sheridan, another CASABLANCA contender, lunches with Ann Sothern (who never lost a role to the Swedish star) and Lamarr.

youthful appearance created a sensation when she made her American debut in *Intermezzo: A Love Story*. So did her acting.

Critics raved about Bergman and little else in the film. They called her incandescent, pure, wholesome, vital, and spiritual. The picture did solid business in the big cities but was a little too sophisticated for other markets.

Bergman returned to Stockholm and her family after completing *Intermezzo* in August. There, she waited anxiously to hear if her American debut had been a success. By the time the film opened in October, however, the world situation made her return to Hollywood doubtful.

Germany already had invaded Czechoslovakia. In November, the Soviet Union invaded Finland. Selznick had no other projects ready, but he worried that if Bergman stayed in Sweden too long, she might be confined to Europe for years. Therefore, he offered to pay her living expenses if she would come to the U.S. as soon as possible.

In December, the Lindstroms embarked

Rick and Ilsa motor through the French countryside in the film's Paris flashback, one of the first scenes shot. What the two had to say to each other is a mystery, as director Michael Curtiz inexplicably forgot to shoot the dialogue written for the scene.

on their own refugee trail. As citizens of a neutral country, they were allowed to travel through the Axis countries, passing through Berlin en route to Genoa, where they embarked for the U.S. on January 2, 1940.

There was little work for Bergman when she arrived. Selznick was still consumed with the national release of *Gone With the Wind* and preparations for his next major production, *Rebecca*. Though he did not have a film for her, he also did not want to lend her out to make a picture that might damage the impression created by *Intermezzo*. Finally, he agreed to let her appear in a Broadway revival of Ferenc Molnar's fantasy *Lilliom*, the play that would provide the source for the Rogers and Hammerstein musical *Carousel* a few years later. She received glowing reviews, but the production had only a limited run.

Selznick turned down a film adaptation of *Victory*, to co-star Fredric March, because the producers would not meet Selznick's asking price of $75,000 for Bergman's services (he only had to pay her $25,000). She herself

turned down an adaptation of Erich Maria Remarque's *So Ends Our Night* because she was afraid the vehemently anti-Nazi story would damage her standing as an international star.

She and Petter were ready to return to Europe when Columbia Pictures finally made a suitable offer—the role of a governess who eventually marries the widowed father of the young boys she had raised in *Adam Had Four Sons*.

She followed almost immediately with MGM's *Rage in Heaven*, another less-than-great role chosen simply to keep her busy. Fortunately, a better role lay around the corner. During the filming of *Intermezzo*, Selznick had shown some of the rushes to Victor Fleming, who was directing *Gone With the Wind* at the time. Fleming was suitably impressed, and when he was planning his next picture, a psychological adaptation of *Dr. Jekyll and Mr. Hyde* to star Spencer Tracy, he asked for Bergman to play the doctor's upper-class fiancée.

Bergman was happy to be working with one of Hollywood's most prominent directors and stars, but disliked the colorless role assigned her. She wanted to play Ivy, the barmaid who becomes involved with the sadistic Mr. Hyde. She proposed switching roles with Lana Turner, who had already been cast as Ivy, and Fleming and Selznick both liked the idea. Bergman stole the film, but it was not a major hit. After a West Coast stage tour in Eugene O'Neill's *Anna Christie*, Selznick could find nothing for her. So she went to Rochester, New York, where her husband had been accepted into medical school.

Then, Bergman found a role she wanted more than any she had ever played before— Maria in Paramount's adaptation of Ernest Hemingway's *For Whom the Bell Tolls*. On her trip from Italy to the U.S., she had met and impressed the great writer's latest wife, Martha Gellhorn. Gellhorn suggested her to Hemingway for the role, which led him to mention her in interviews as a possibility.

Paramount was not prepared to offer such a plum role to an actress under contract

Does he or doesn't he? Did she or didn't she? Victor (Paul Henreid) prepares to leave for the resistance meeting. Although he never says it directly, his behavior indicates that he has deduced the truth about Rick and Ilsa's relationship. Bergman would later claim she shot this scene without knowing which man she would end up with.

elsewhere. Bergman's name joined a long list of contenders that included contract players Paulette Goddard and Betty Field. She even did a test for the role, though at Selznick's insistence, it was only a brief, silent piece designed to see how she looked in a short wig. But director Sam Wood complained that she was too tall to play the innocent young resistance fighter and that she was too heavy to look good in slacks.

Bergman's campaign to play Maria coincided with Wallis's search for someone to play Ilsa, and while there was any chance of her landing the role in *For Whom the Bell Tolls*, the last thing Selznick wanted to do was tie her down with another commitment. So he avoided Wallis.

Meanwhile, Wallis considered two other actresses. He was impressed with Edwige Feuillière's performance in the French film *Sarajevo*, but the "first lady of the French screen," as she was called, was in Europe for the duration. Michelle Morgan had scored a hit as a young innocent drawn into the resis-

Paul Henreid (opposite) exuded continental charm so strong, few questioned his casting as an American architect in NOW, VOYAGER. This Bette Davis vehicle about the joys of romance, dieting, and psychoanalysis seemed to set him firmly on the road to stardom.

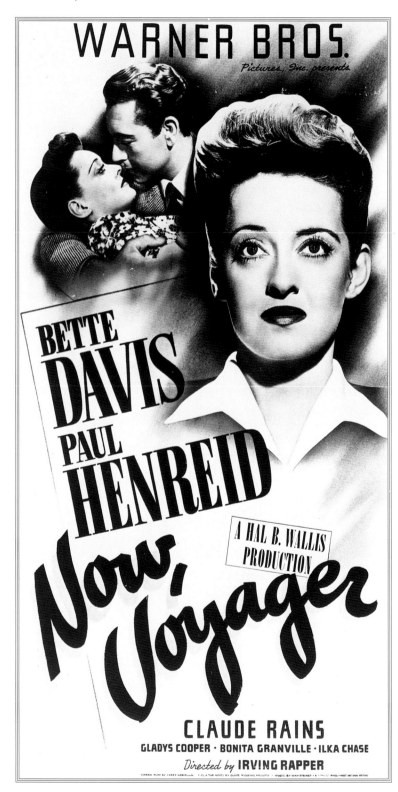

WARNER BROS.
Pictures, Inc. presents

BETTE
DAVIS
PAUL
HENREID

A HAL B. WALLIS
PRODUCTION

Now,
Voyager

CLAUDE RAINS
GLADYS COOPER · BONITA GRANVILLE · ILKA CHASE
Directed by IRVING RAPPER

tance in RKO's *Joan of Paris*, but her asking price was $55,000. Nonetheless, she was tested on April 9.

Tired of being stonewalled by Selznick, Wallis followed him everywhere—finally catching up with him in New York's Hotel Carlyle. By this time, Norwegian ballerina Vera Zorina had won the role in *For Whom the Bell Tolls*, and Bergman was desperate to find a picture, any picture. So, Selznick agreed to let the Epsteins tell him the story.

The Epsteins approached their meeting with Selznick with some trepidation, as they had only completed the first third of the script and had not even Europeanized the leading lady. But Wallis's faith in their ability to improvise proved well founded. The writers met with Selznick and began describing the action, fleshing it out with lines and bits they had already created. Then, they said the magic word— *Algiers*. Selznick agreed to discuss terms for a loan-out.

By April 14, Selznick had agreed to loan Bergman to Warner Bros. for $25,000. In return, he would borrow Olivia de Havilland from them for the same price. Selznick eventually sold the de Havilland portion of the deal to RKO, where she made the forgettable comedy *Government Girl* with Sonny Tufts.

I f getting Bergman for *Casablanca* was difficult, finding the right Victor was next to impossible. There were two actors Wallis had in mind: Philip Dorn, who had appeared in Warners' *Underground*, and Paul Henreid, who had been borrowed from RKO for the Bette Davis vehicle *Now, Voyager*. There were problems with both actors. Dorn was under contract to MGM, and on April 14, Wallis was notified that the studio planned to use him in the Greer Garson– Ronald Colman tearjerker *Random Harvest*. Henreid, on the other hand, was available, but far from interested.

Wallis states in his autobiography that Henreid hated the role, claiming that "an

underground leader who appeared in a white tropical suit and hat in a famous nightclub and talked openly with Nazis was ridiculous and redolent of musical comedy." Also, Henreid was very clearly on the star track thanks to his roles in *Joan of Paris* and the upcoming *Now, Voyager*. He felt, justifiably, that Victor was secondary in importance to Rick, and that the role could forestall his career.

Although Paul George Julius von Henreid initially turned down the role of Victor Laszlo, there was some similarity between actor and character. Like Laszlo, Henreid was a refugee from the Third Reich and, like the character, he also was a vehement opponent of Naziism.

The actor was born in Trieste, Austria-Hungary, in 1908, the son of a noble family with connections to the banking business. World War I triggered a major decline in the von Henreids' fortunes, and they moved to Vienna, where Paul's interest in the arts eventually led him to a position in publishing.

But the young Henreid dreamed of becoming an actor. In 1933, he managed to impress Otto Preminger, who at that time was managing director for the great Max Reinhardt. Henreid enrolled in Reinhardt's acting school and eventually began building a following as a young leading man. He made his film debut in a 1935 Austrian picture called *Jersey Lilly*.

In 1937, Henreid went to England to play Prince Albert opposite Anna Neagle in *Victoria the Great*. He also re-created his role in *The Jersey Lilly* for the London stage, becoming a bonafide matinee idol.

When Hitler took Austria in 1938, it became dangerous for Henreid to return home. His prominent work in England, his family's position, and his outspoken anti-Nazi sentiments put his life at risk. When war broke out in 1939, the United Kingdom's government issued orders to round up German, Austrian, and Italian citizens, and Henreid was in danger of deportation.

Fortunately, his colleagues in the British theater, including future on-screen enemy Conrad Veidt, convinced the government to reclassify him. He was forced to remain under surveillance, but at least he was safe in England for the time being.

Victoria the Great had been a big hit in England and brought Henreid two other films that introduced him to American audiences. *Goodbye Mr. Chips* was, in fact, an American production, filmed by MGM at their Pinewood Studios. It also was a major success in the States, winning Robert Donat the Oscar for Best Actor of 1939 and making Greer Garson a star. The following year, Henreid played a major role in Sir Carol Reed's *Night Train*, considered one of the greatest espionage thrillers ever made.

Henreid's screen exposure paid off in 1940, when he was invited to appear on Broadway, once again as star of *The Jersey Lilly*. The offer was a godsend, freeing him from the constant fear that a change in British government policy could send him back to face possible death in Austria. Henreid arrived in the U.S. to begin work with stage legend Katherine Cornell and producer Gilbert Miller, but the production was cancelled. The setback was only temporary, however, as Henreid's film credits won him representation from agent Lew Wasserman at MCA.

Wasserman helped Henreid land a contract at RKO, where he made his American screen debut in 1942 appropriately cast as a resistance fighter in *Joan of Paris*. The picture was far from a hit commercially, but it did a great deal for leading lady Michelle Morgan and a young supporting actor named Alan Ladd, as well as for Henreid. With his dark good looks, an intriguingly romantic accent, some well-written action scenes, and a suitably macho black leather jacket, the star made a solid impression on female audience members and more than one producer, including Hal Wallis.

Wallis was about to embark on his first independent production under a new contract

The screenwriters added a scene with a resistance member (John Qualen, above right) to strengthen Victor's position in the underground, but other scenes, like Victor and Ilsa's visit with Señor Ferrari (Sydney Greenstreet, opposite right), underlined the character's helplessness.

with Warner Bros., an adaptation of the Olive Higgins Prouty best seller *Now, Voyager*. Bette Davis was set to star as a frumpy, middle-aged neurotic transformed into a glamorous woman of the world by psychiatry and a fashion makeover. Wallis needed an actor strong enough to hold his own against her and someone whose screen image would represent the epitome of romance. When Wallis saw *Joan of Paris*, he knew he had found a suitable match for his star.

Henreid's scenes with Davis smoldered, and the actor's light Viennese accent added a special air of intrigue to the performance. In addition, Henreid created a bit of business that would become a part of motion-picture history.

In Prouty's novel, the lovers have a special way of lighting their cigarettes that writer Casey Robinson preserved in the adaptation. It was a complicated process involving passing two cigarettes and one match back and forth ad infinitum. But when Davis and Henreid tried it on the soundstage, there was never enough dialogue, or enough match, for the business to work. Finally, Henreid suggested something he and his wife did while driving together—she would place two cigarettes in her mouth, light them, and place one between his lips. On the road, it was a practicality. When Henreid did it on screen, it was magic.

With strong performances in two leading romantic roles, Henreid seemed destined to become a major star. The last thing he needed was the second male lead in what looked to him like a minor suspense story.

So, Wallis considered every option he could think of. He tried to get Nils Asther, who had played an Oriental warlord to Barbara Stanwyck's missionary in *The Bitter Tea of General Yen*, but Asther had signed to appear in some films for Pine-Thomas, a B-movie unit attached to Paramount. Jean-Pierre Aumont, a French actor who had recently emi-

grated to the U.S., was tested, but Wallis thought he was too young. The producer was interested in Joseph Cotten, another Selznick contractee, who had just appeared with Merle Oberon in *Lydia*, but there is no record of Wallis's pursuing the matter beyond an initial query about Cotten's fee. By April 22, Wallis advised Michael Curtiz that in lieu of anyone else, they would probably have to consider such solid, if unexciting, character types as Dean Jagger, Ian Hunter, or Herbert Marshall. Then, global events intervened.

With American entry into World War II, the U.S. government went about rounding up enemy aliens. People of Japanese lineage were sent to containment camps, while those of German birth had to demonstrate their loyalty or face deportation. Because Austria had, at least ostensibly, accepted membership in the Third Reich, the Austrian-born Henreid set out to secure a contract with a studio powerful enough to keep him in the U.S. He had already signed with RKO, but the strength of his work in *Now, Voyager* made it possible for his agent to get Warners to pick up part of his contract. An agreement was reached allowing Warner Bros. to use him in three films per year and RKO in one.

Henreid was approached once more about appearing in *Casablanca*. He asked that the part be beefed up and that he be given co-star billing with Bogart and Bergman. According to legend, he also insisted that he get Bergman in the end, though considering that no mention of this stipulation appears in Henreid's legal files and that Wallis and the writers later considered alternate endings leaving Bergman with Bogart at the final fadeout, this seems highly unlikely. On May 1, 1942, less than a month before shooting was scheduled to begin, Wallis agreed to build up the part and guarantee Henreid star billing.

OPPOSITE: Nothing in the film gave Henreid the opportunity to be as forceful as he appears in this publicity shot. BELOW: Victor quietly urges Rick to join the resistance.

C.617

Chapter Three

PERHAPS

Tomorrow We'll Be On That

PLANE

Perhaps the best actor in CASABLANCA's cast, Claude Rains as the Vichy police captain Louis Renault. The role had been shaped for him by writers Julius J. and Philip G. Epstein, who regarded him as their good-luck charm after his success in Julius's FOUR DAUGHTERS.

One of the key factors in *Casablanca*'s success is the superb supporting cast brought on board by Hal Wallis, which had a texture, an intangible rightness, rarely duplicated on-screen. Part of this texture is the assemblage of dialects—Sydney Greenstreet's cultured stage tones, Claude Rains's British enunciation, S. Z. Sakall's Hungarian. The Warners Publicity Department would boast that the cast included thirty-four nationalities.

Representing England was Claude Rains, the only actor ever considered to play Renault. The distinguished character actor had first performed on stage in 1900, at the age of eleven. After serving as a leading man for the Theatre Guild on Broadway in the twenties, Rains traveled to Hollywood, but was hardly seen in his film debut in 1933 when he played the title role in Universal's *The Invisible Man*.

Rains quickly became a Hollywood rarity, a character lead—someone who could carry a picture in a nontraditional role or bolster a film with a meaty supporting performance. He arrived at Warner Bros. in 1935 with a four-picture deal, making his studio debut as the villain in *Anthony Adverse*. That set the tone for his appearances in such early Warners' pictures as *The Prince and the Pauper*, *The Adventures of Robin Hood*, and *The Sea Hawk*.

In 1938, Rains also demonstrated his skill at playing more benign parts when he was cast as the classical musician raising *Four Daughters* with wife Fay Bainter in one of Jack Warner's favorite films. A year later, on loan to Columbia as the corrupt senator in *Mr. Smith Goes to Washington*, Rains won the first of four Oscar nominations for Best Supporting Actor (he would never actually win). He also won the right to expand his career beyond Warners' Burbank studios.

Rains negotiated a new contract in 1940 requiring only two films per year at Warners and allowing him to make two films of his choosing at other studios. He returned to Columbia to play the heavenly bureaucrat in *Here Comes Mr. Jordan* and to Universal as Lon Chaney, Jr.'s father in *The Wolfman*. At Warners, he was the only actor good enough to pull off the demanding role of the brooding Dr. Tower in *Kings Row*.

Rains was a frequent performer in Hal Wallis's films, so it was only natural that the producer should cast him in his first independent picture, *Now, Voyager*. That was the actor's first 1942 assignment at Warners. The second came when the Epstein brothers decided to turn Luis Rinaldo in *Everybody Comes to Rick's* into Captain Renault of *Casablanca*.

One of the great ironies in *Casablanca*'s casting is the fact that the film's Nazi villain was portrayed by one of Hollywood's staunchest enemies of the Nazi movement, German actor Conrad Veidt. There was nothing offensive about such casting in Veidt's eyes, however. In fact, he insisted on it.

Veidt was born near Berlin, where he studied with Max Reinhardt before making his stage debut in 1913. Despite distinguished stage beginnings, it was film that would provide his greatest successes. Veidt began making movies in 1917. Two years later he became an international sensation as Cesare the somnambulist in the breakthrough German expressionist picture *The Cabinet of Dr. Caligari.*

Caligari was a hit around the world. In many countries, it was the first German film imported since World War I. Success at home led to roles in other countries. Veidt made three films in the U.S. during the silent era and was invited to make films in England, which proved to be a godsend. Not only was the actor an outspoken critic of the Third Reich, he was married to a Jewish woman. He stayed in England from the mid-thirties and returned to Germany only once, in 1938. But the visit was a colossal

mistake. The government immediately tried to keep him there, issuing a cover story that he was too ill to travel. Only a contingent of doctors sent by Gaumont British Studios, which had Veidt under contract, got him back to England. Wary of repeating the situation, Veidt became a British citizen in 1939, when he was cast as the villainous vizier in producer Alexander Korda's epic remake of *The Thief of Bagdad.* When wartime strictures forced the production to move to Hollywood, Veidt went with it—and stayed.

The U.S. seemed the safest place for Veidt and his wife to spend the war years, and with the rise of interest in war subjects, there was a demand for German-born actors to play enemy roles. In fact, when Veidt signed his

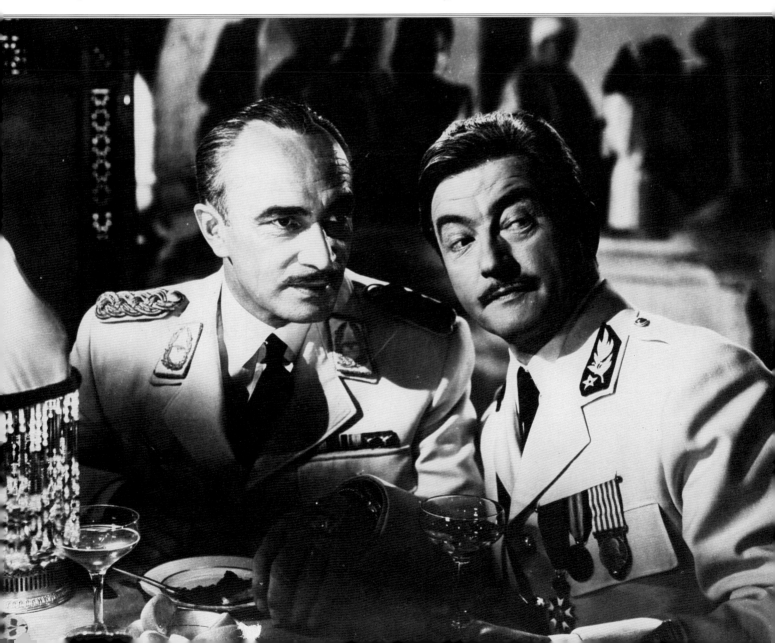

CONRAD VEIDT
C.565

contract with MGM, he demanded a clause stating that he would only play villains. Such parts made his fortune on-screen, and more importantly, he felt the best way to fight the Nazis in Germany was by portraying them unsympathetically in Hollywood.

Veidt's villains were unlike the stock Prussian martinets played by so many lesser actors. His Nazis were not crude and loud, but rather more cultured sorts whose refinement masked their evil souls. He had so much continental charm in such roles, in fact, that after menacing Norma Shearer in *Escape*, Humphrey Bogart in *All Through the Night*, and, in a less political role, Joan Crawford in *A Woman's Face*, the actor began receiving letters from romantically inclined fans. It was that smoothness that helped Veidt beat out former Burnett and Allison associate Otto Preminger for the role of Strasser. The $5,000 per week that MGM demanded for Veidt's services made him one of the highest-paid cast members.

Another important supporting role—Señor Ferrari, king of the Black Market and proprietor of the Blue Parrot—functions as a dark mirror of Rick and required an actor capable of marrying a charming, almost jovial exterior with a more sinister side. Wallis knew that Sydney Greenstreet was the perfect man for the role. He even agreed to the actor's demands for more money—$3,750 per week—and ordered the Epsteins to expand the part to suit the talents of the corpulent actor who had delayed his screen debut until his sixty-first year.

The Greenstreets could trace their roots to the Norman conquest, and Greenstreet grew up in the 400-year-old family manse in Kent. His childhood playground was some nearby Roman ruins. The male Greenstreets had a long tradition of working in the leather business, but Sydney was rebel enough to go off in search of adventure, taking a job with a tea company in Ceylon.

But life in the tea trade had its boring stretches, during which the young man amused himself by reading the complete works of Shakespeare. Before he could memorize every line, however, a drought ended his first career and he returned to England.

Through a variety of other jobs, Greenstreet realized that his real dream was acting. He used his wages to finance dramatic training and made his stage debut at the age of twenty-three, aptly cast as a murderer in *Sherlock Holmes*. His acting teacher, Ben Greet, was putting together a U.S. tour in 1904 and cast Greenstreet along with a rising young actress named Sybil Thorndike. After making his Broadway debut with the company in *Everyman*, Greenstreet decided to make New York his home.

The young actor was surprisingly versatile, and his impressive girth made him a natural for strong supporting roles. He worked with some of the finest actors of the early twentieth century. No less a light

With the outbreak of World War II, Conrad Veidt specialized in playing Nazis like Major Strasser (opposite), but his typecasting as a villain actually began with his first major screen hit, as Cesare the somnambulist (below) in the breakthrough expressionist horror film THE CABINET OF DR. CALIGARI.

than Sir Herbert Beerbohm Tree hailed Greenstreet as the greatest featured actor of his day.

After three decades playing the classics, Greenstreet moved into musical comedy, co-starring with Bob Hope in the original production of *Roberta*. He might have stayed in that lucrative branch of show business longer, but he caught the attention of Alfred Lunt and Lynn Fontanne, and began appearing regularly in their productions—*The Sea Gull*, *The Taming of the Shrew*, *Amphytrion '38*, *Idiot's Delight*, and *There Shall Be No Night*. At the time, the Lunts praised him as the only actor capable of matching their trademark delivery of natural, overlapping dialogue.

It was while Greenstreet was appearing with the Lunts in the Los Angeles company of

Although the role of Señor Ferrari was relatively small, Warners' publicity shots for CASABLANCA took full advantage of Sydney Greenstreet's menacing presence (right), as in this shot with Joy Page and Helmut Dantine.

There Shall Be No Night that John Huston saw the production and realized that he had found the perfect actor to play the civilized, venal Kaspar Guttman in *The Maltese Falcon*. So, at sixty-one, Greenstreet made his screen debut opposite Humphrey Bogart and Mary Astor, winning rave reviews and an Oscar nomination for Best Supporting Actor.

The role also brought him a contract at Warner Bros., where he settled in as a character lead second in prominence only to Claude Rains. Greenstreet had a popular on-screen reunion with Bogart, whom he left trussed up next to a burning keg of dynamite in *Across the Pacific*, before Wallis decided to bring the two actors together a third time, across the Atlantic in *Casablanca*.

A Man of Substance

ydney Greenstreet's size was his fortune, as well as the source of several anecdotes of near legendary stature. Through his career, he tried to maintain an average weight of 280 pounds, though at times he mushroomed to 325. During his days of theatrical touring, he boasted that he had broken one out of every five hotel beds he had slept in. When the script of one of his Warner Bros. films required him to play a scene in a telephone booth, he became so firmly stuck that the booth finally had to be taken apart.

But the greatest story about Greenstreet's weight took place during an outdoor performance of Shakespeare's *As You Like It*. The actor was cast as the good Duke Senior, and in the middle of his second scene, the three-foot-high platform stage collapsed beneath him. He always refused to take credit for bringing down the stage. But his next lines brought down the house. When the audience stopped laughing, he emerged from the cave-in to state, "True it is, we have seen better days," setting off another gale of laughter. His next line stopped the show: "Sit you down in gentleness."

Sydney Greenstreet (below). His girth helped him win the plum role of Casper Gutman, nicknamed "The Fat Man," in THE MALTESE FALCON (below left, seated).

If the *Casablanca* cast did indeed comprise thirty-four nationalities, half that number could be found on Peter Lorre's resumé. The accomplished actor was born Laszlo Löwenstein in Rosenberg, Hungary, in 1904 and turned to acting when his first career choice, psychiatry, failed to satisfy him. Although he had studied with the pioneers in the field, Sigmund Freud and Alfred Adler, he did not have the patience to listen to patients all day. In fact, with his manic sense of humor, Lorre found most of their revelations highly amusing.

With a colleague, Lorre pioneered in the development of psychodrama, even mounting a theatrical production based on his patients' acting out of their problems. The project failed, but Lorre found that he loved performing for an audience. A theatrical producer from Breslau, Poland, saw the production and offered Lorre a job.

From Poland, Lorre moved to theaters in Austria, Switzerland, and Germany, where he also started appearing in films in 1928. Three years later, Fritz Lang cast him as a fictionalized version of brutal serial-killer Peter Kurten. The resultant film, *M*, has been hailed as one of the greatest motion pictures of all time. It brought Lorre international acclaim, which he almost did not live to enjoy when a crowd, convinced

Menace was Peter Lorre's stock in trade through more than three decades of movies. He made his U.S. film debut in MAD LOVE (opposite), playing a surgeon who grafts the hands of a murderer to the wrists of an injured pianist (Colin Clive), then tries to drive his patient mad in order to steal the man's wife (Frances Drake). Lorre's presence alone was enough to add to a film's tension, as demonstrated by the strong impression he made in the relatively small role of black marketeer Guillermo Ugarte in CASABLANCA (below). Other films during his stay at Warner Bros. included THE BEAST WITH FIVE FINGERS, THE MASK OF DIMITRIOS, CONFIDENTIAL AGENT, THREE STRANGERS and ARSENIC AND OLD LACE, in which he spoofed his image.

he really was the character, stoned him in Berlin.

The actor made his first English film for Alfred Hitchcock, playing the head of the spy ring in the original version of *The Man Who Knew Too Much*. He also accepted offers to work in the U.S., where he debuted as the demented scientist in *Mad Love*, a remake of *The Hands of Orlac*. After another Hitchcock film in England, *Secret Agent*, Lorre decided to settle permanently in America.

He starred as Oriental detective Mr. Moto in a series of eight low-budget films at 20th Century–Fox. He hated the role, but it served its purpose financially, even if many audience members were now convinced that he was Japanese. After more work as a free agent, including the memorable RKO thriller *The Stranger on the Third Floor*, in which he played yet another demented killer, Lorre settled into a seven-year contract at Warner Bros.

Initially, Jack Warner had no great plans for him. He was hired to play stock heavies, and even those were few and far between because of his typecasting in the Mr. Moto films. Then John Huston gave him the role of Joel Cairo, the effeminate killer in *The Maltese Falcon*. It introduced Lorre to his perfect on-screen co-star, Sydney Greenstreet, and his perfect off-screen drinking companion, Humphrey Bogart. After a reunion with Bogie in *All Through the Night*, Lorre was a natural choice to join the cast of *Casablanca*, though, like Greenstreet, he too held out for more money—$1,750 per week.

Of all the key players in *Casablanca*, only one had been to the actual city, Arthur "Dooley" Wilson, who played Sam. Young Arthur Wilson entered show business in 1901 at the age of seven, after his father's death. Wilson had a strong singing voice and went to work performing in tent shows and at church meetings. After several years of one-night stands and minstrel shows, Wilson's travels brought him to Chicago, where he joined the Pekin Stock Company, an all-black theater, and began performing in repertory. The dearth of plays about black life at the time meant donning white face for many of the shows. While working in Chicago, he also learned to play the drums.

From Chicago, Wilson moved to New York and steady work in Harlem's night spots. By the twenties, he formed a band, the Red Devils, to tour Europe. They were a huge hit there, where jazz was an obsession, and no color bar held them back. In Casablanca, they performed at a soirée in honor of World War I hero T. E. Lawrence.

But late in the decade, homesickness led Wilson back to the U.S., where he used musical jobs to support himself while he tried to move into acting. With the paucity of good roles for black actors, it would take almost a decade. His big break finally came in the late thirties with a role in *Of Mice and Men* on tour.

Then, he heard of an all-black musical being cast in New York.

Play it Again—Molly

Dooley Wilson's stage name hit just the right note for the young actor. While performing in white-face with the all-black Pekin Stock Company, Arthur Wilson developed a special flair for Irish roles because of his surprisingly natural brogue. He made such a hit playing a leprechaun who sang the song "Mr. Dooley," that he adopted the title for his professional name. The theater and film worlds can be grateful that the song was not "Mother Machree" or "Sweet Molly Malone."

It might have been "Molly" Wilson tickling the ivories in CASABLANCA. For that matter, the performer might have been female in more than name; Hal Wallis considered Lena Horne, Ella Fitzgerald, and Hazel Scott for the role.

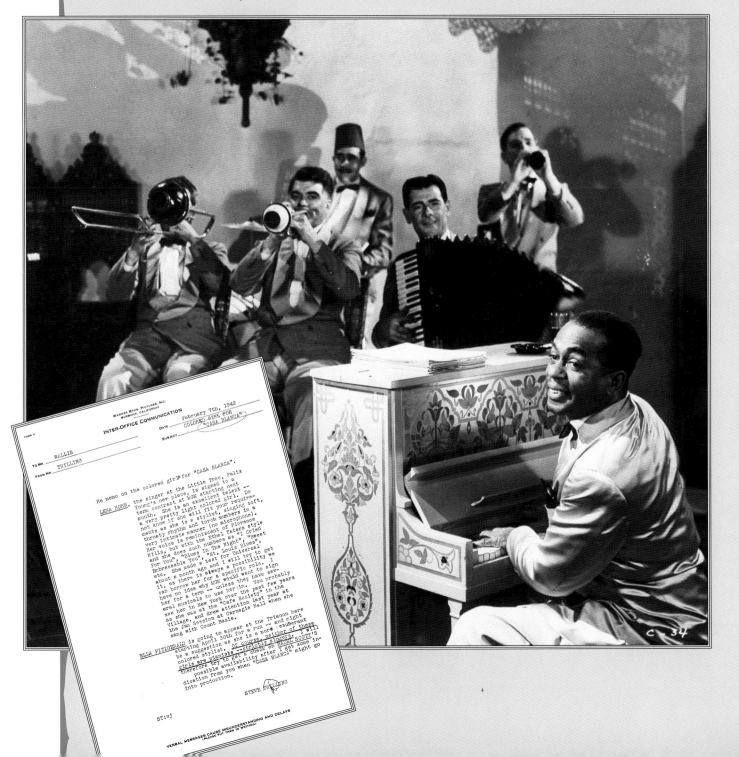

WARNER BROS. PICTURES, INC.
BURBANK, CALIFORNIA

FORM 11

INTER-OFFICE COMMUNICATION

DATE February 7th, 1942

SUBJECT COLORED GIRL FOR "CASA BLANCA"

TO MR. WALLIS

FROM MR. TRILLING

Re memo on the colored girls for "CASA BLANCA".

LENA HORNE, the singer at the Little Troc, Felix Young's new place, is signed to a term contract at MGM starting next month. She is an excellent talent -- a very pretty light colored girl. Do not know if she will fit your requirements as she is a stylist, singing soft, throaty Rhythm and torch numbers in a very intimate manner (no microphone). Her voice is reminiscent of Florence Mills, but with the Ethel Waters style and she does such numbers as "I Cried For You", "Blues In The Night", "Sweet Embraceable You", "St. Louis Blues", etc. She made a test for Universal about a month ago and I will try to get it, as there is always a possibility we can borrow her for a specific role. You have no idea why MGM would want to sign her for a term -- unless they have several musicals to use her in. You probably saw her in New York over the past few years as she was at the "Cafe Society" in the Village, and drew attention last year at the Jam Session at Carnegie Hall when she sang with Count Basie.

ELLA FITZGERALD is going to appear at the Trianon here starting April 30th for a run -- and might be a suggestion as she is a more exuberant colored stylist -- strictly singer. I will therefore try to get a check on HAZEL SCOTT'S possible availability after I get some indication from you when "CASA BLANCA" might go into production.

STEVE TRILLING

STrvj

VERBAL MESSAGES CAUSE MISUNDERSTANDING AND DELAYS
(PLEASE PUT THEM IN WRITING)

The man caught between S. Z. Sakall (left) and Leonid Kinsky's clowning doesn't know how lucky he is. In early drafts of the screenplay, Sascha (Kinsky) was supposed to practice bartending American style by unknowingly mixing up a Mickey Finn and serving it to one of the German officers.

He auditioned hoping to get a small role and was hired as Little Joe, the star of *Cabin in the Sky*. Though he lost the film version to Eddie "Rochester" Anderson, a more recognizable name on the strength of his performances on "The Jack Benny Show," the play was Wilson's ticket to Hollywood. He signed a contract at Paramount, but they only offered him what he called "pullman-porter" roles in films like *My Favorite Blonde* and *Night in New Orleans*. He was on the verge of leaving, and Paramount was ready to let his option lapse, when he got word of the audition for *Casablanca*.

Had Wallis followed his initial impulse about the role, however, Wilson would not have had a chance. During a trip to New York, the producer visited the Cafe Uptown Society and was impressed with the performance of singer-pianist Hazel Scott. On February 5, he wrote to Steve Trilling suggesting they make Sam a woman. In addition to Scott, Wallis asked Trilling to inquire about the availability of Ella Fitzgerald and Lena Horne.

Somewhere along the line, this idea was abandoned. In April, Michael Curtiz directed Dooley Wilson and Clarence Muse in tests for the role. Wallis liked both tests, though he felt Curtiz had made Wilson's test too comical. More problematic was the fact that Wilson could not play the piano.

On May 1, Wallis told Trilling to hire Muse for the role. But two days later, the studio's general counsel, R. J. Obringer, issued a memo stating that Wilson would play Sam. There is no recorded reason for this change of heart. Perhaps, because Muse was under contract to MGM, Wallis could not negotiate a satisfactory loan-out deal. In his autobiography, Wallis says that he decided against Muse because he felt his portrayal was too stereotyped. It is possible that, after Wallis settled on Muse as the choice, he was influenced by others on the lot. In particular, Howard Koch, who was already doing rewrites on *Casablanca*, had a reputation for sensitivity on racial issues, as demonstrated by his handling of the black characters played by Ernest Anderson and Hattie McDaniel in *In This Our Life*.

Whatever the reason, Wilson won the role. Warners agreed to pay Paramount $500 a week for Wilson's services over a seven-week period. Only $150 of that weekly check would go to Wilson.

To supply comic relief from the problems of the main story line, Hal Wallis turned to another refugee from Hitler's Europe, S. Z. Sakall, a comedic actor whose lovable, excitable screen characters would eventually earn him the nickname "Cuddles." The "S. Z.," by the way, came not from Sakall's given name, Eugene Gero, but from his professional name in Europe, "Szöke."

The character actor had begun his career on stage and in silent films in Hungary and Germany, but he did not hit his stride until the coming of sound made him a comic star in the latter country. Unfortunately, the coming of the Third Reich also made him persona non grata there. After a few films in Hungary and Austria, he fled to the U.S., making his American film debut in 1940 opposite Deanna Durbin in *It's a Date*.

Sakall's first big U.S. hit was *Ball of Fire*, a popular 1942 comedy starring Gary Cooper and Barbara Stanwyck. The film was actually an updated version of "Snow White and the Seven Dwarfs," with Sakall, Richard Haydn, and Oskar Homolka among the dwarfs. The same year, Sakall signed a contract with Warner Bros., where he would remain until the fifties. His first picture under contract was another hit, *Yankee Doodle Dandy*.

When he was first offered the role of Carl in *Casablanca*, he hated it and turned it down, as did several other character comedians. *Casablanca* went into production with the role still uncast. When Wallis's back was against the wall, Sakall finally agreed to play the role—if the studio would guarantee him four weeks' work. This was twice what he had gotten on his

When he began making films in the U.S., S. Z. Sakall's benign smile and pinchable jowls earned him the nickname "Cuddles," which often turned up in the credits of his American films, though not in those for CASABLANCA, where he was erroneously billed as "S. K. Sakall."

previous pictures and much more time than Wallis anticipated using him. Finally, the producer compromised with a three-week minimum on Sakall's weekly salary of $1,750.

To play Sakall's partner in comedy, Sascha the bartender, Wallis considered several actors, including George Tobias, who would later star on television's "Bewitched" as next-door-neighbor Abner Kravitz. His final choice was Leonid Kinsky. The comic player was a refugee, too, but from the Russian Revolution. After turning to acting, he worked throughout Europe and South America before settling in Hollywood in the thirties. Kinsky made his film debut in director Ernst Lubitsch's 1932 comic classic *Trouble in Paradise*, with Herbert Marshall, Miriam Hopkins, and Kay Francis. Then he went on to supply an international flavor in such films as *Peter Ibbetson*, with Gary Cooper; *Les Miserables*, with Fredric March and Charles Laughton; *The General Died at Dawn*, with Cooper, Madeleine Carroll, and Akim Tamiroff; and *That Night in Rio*, with Alice Faye, Don Ameche, and Carmen Miranda.

The Warner Bros. Public Relations Department made a great deal out of the South American background of Corinna Mura, who had been hired to play Andrea, the female singer at Rick's Café. But Warners never mentioned which South American country Mura hailed from for one simple reason—she didn't.

The singer-guitar player was born Corinna Wall in San Antonio, Texas, to a Spanish-English father and Scottish mother. Wall's parents wanted her to have a musical career but were so upset at her decision to sing pop rather than grand opera that they had her committed to a rest home in Connecticut. She learned to play Spanish guitar from a fellow inmate, and that led ironically to a career in nightclubs. She starred in her own radio show, "The Corinna Mura International Salon," before making her film debut with a singing role in *Call Out the Marines*. *Casablanca* was her second picture.

For Jan and Annina Brandel (the name had been changed from Viereck in the original), the young couple whose plight spurs Rick into action, Wallis cast Helmut Dantine and Joy Page. Dantine, an Austrian, was yet another fugitive from Hitler and had just scored a hit as the downed German flyer in MGM's *Mrs. Miniver*. Page was a recent addition to the contract-players list at Warners and had a special in with the boss. Jack Warner had recently married her mother. *Casablanca* would mark the start of her brief film career, which ended when she married future Warners executive Bill Orr.

To play Rick's rejected lady, Yvonne, Wallis signed Madeleine LeBeau, a nineteen-year-old French refugee who had made her film debut in *Hold Back the Dawn*. Also in that film was German Curt Bois, who had a plum cameo in *Casablanca* as the pickpocket labeled "The Dark European." Canadian John Qualen—who played Berger, Victor Laszlo's resistance contact in Casablanca—had already had a long career playing immigrants in such films as *Street Scene* and *Our Daily Bread*, in addition to parts in two important John Ford films, *The*

The singer played by Corinna Mura (center) was typical of the many Latin American characters featured in Hollywood's wartime product to appeal to the new foreign markets opening up south of the border. The actress would play similar roles in PASSAGE TO MARSEILLES and HONEYMOON before leaving films in 1947.

Grapes of Wrath and *The Long Voyage Home*. Qualen's most famous role, however, was as the framed death-row inmate saved by Rosalind Russell and Cary Grant in *His Girl Friday*.

The staff at Rick's place was rounded out by Dan Seymour, a 300-pound actor who billed himself as "the young Sydney Greenstreet," as Rick's Arab doorman and bodyguard, Abdul; and noted French actor Marcel Dalio, the star of Jean Renoir's *La Grande Illusion* and *Les Regles du Jeu*, as the croupier. Dalio had barely escaped from France with his life after the German invasion, and while spending the war years in Hollywood, he learned that his parents had died in a concentration camp.

The same year *Casablanca* premiered, Ludwig Stossel—cast as Sakall's refugee friend Mr. Leuchtag—played Gary Cooper's father in *Pride of the Yankees*. Mrs. Leuchtag was played by Ilka Gruning, who had also appeared in Warners' 1941 anti-Nazi drama, *Underground*. The street vendor who tries to overcharge Ilsa was played by the Italian Frank Puglia, a one-time opera singer whose American film career dated back to D. W. Griffith's *Orphans of the Storm*.

Faces of the dispossessed: (opposite) French refugee Madeleine LeBeau as Yvonne, (right) Austrian refugee Helmut Dantine as Jan Brandel, and (center) Joy Page as Annina. Of the three, Page probably had it the easiest: she was the boss's stepdaughter. Dantine had the most lasting career, usually cast as a Nazi throughout the 1940s.

Lining up behind-the-camera talent appears to have gone pretty smoothly except for two instances where Wallis failed to get his first choice. To direct, he went after one of the best in the business, William Wyler. Apparently Wyler never even got around to reading the script Wallis sent him in February 1942.

With Wyler either unavailable or uninterested, Wallis logically turned to Michael Curtiz, the number-one director on the Warners lot. Curtiz had already responded favorably to the script, and his own experience, having emigrated from his native Hungary during World War I, made him ideally suited to *Casablanca*'s depiction of life on the refugee trail. He also still had family in Hungary. In fact, during one of Jack Warner's annual European vacations, the studio chief had, at Curtiz's request, visited these overseas relations to make sure they were doing well and encourage them to emigrate to the U.S. Curtiz was one of the few people at the studio who could command such loyalty from Warner.

He was born Mihály Kertész in Budapest on Christmas Eve 1888. Young Mihály went to work at an early age, finding employment as an extra at various theaters around Vienna, where the family had moved in search of better prospects. At the age of sixteen, he joined the circus, saving his earnings so he could attend the Royal Academy of Theatre and Art in Budapest. That led to stage work and, eventually, the screen. But Curtiz found no great challenge in playing short scenes for the camera, certainly nothing to compare with performing a full-length play for a live audience. In 1912, he signed to make some films for a Hungarian studio that, to save money, had not bothered hiring a director. With nobody to tell the actors what to do, Curtiz took over. Although he was not credited on screen, the

Michael Curtiz's position as the top director on the Warners lot is attested to by this full-page ad in the 1943 "Film Yearbook." The copy reads "If you're looking for the best, turn to Warner Bros.!" They might have added, "If you're looking for Warners' best, turn to Curtiz!"

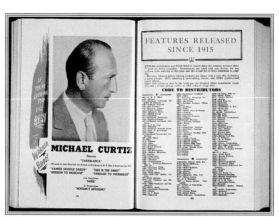

films *The Last Bohemian* and *Today and Tomorrow* are considered his first directing jobs.

Having stumbled into a more interesting line of work, Curtiz was determined to learn the tricks of the trade. He traveled to Sweden to work with Victor Sjöström, who was already earning a reputation as Europe's greatest filmmaker.

Curtiz was doing well in Sweden and had started directing his own projects when World War I broke out. He returned home to serve in the Austro-Hungarian cavalry and even worked for a while making propaganda films for the government. When peace came, though there is no record of why, Curtiz was forced to flee to Germany.

There he found work at the famed UFA studios, home of Fritz Lang and Robert Wiene. Like them, he was heavily influenced by the German expressionists and developed an aptitude for using shadow and light to intensify the mood of a story. Among his most successful efforts were historical pieces, including two biblical epics: *The Queen of Sin and the Spectacle of Sodom and Gomorrah* and *Moon Over Israel*. The latter film (though never released in the U.S. because Paramount bought it and locked it away to avoid comparison with Cecil B. De Mille's *The Ten Commandments*) was the impetus behind Curtiz's American career.

Harry Warner was visiting Europe in the mid-twenties when he saw Curtiz at work and was suitably impressed. He offered the young director a contract and brought him to Warner Bros. in 1926. Curtiz was lucky enough to arrive in Hollywood during the heyday of silent films, so his limited command of English was no hindrance at first. By the time sound arrived he was able to deal with the subtleties of screen dialogue.

Curtiz worked in every genre at the studio. With his early exposure to expressionism, he brought a special dark side to such crime dramas as *20,000 Years in Sing Sing* and Warners' infrequent forays into the horror field—*The Mad Genius, Dr. X, The Mystery of the Wax Museum,* and *The Walking Dead.* When Warners was ready to move into bigger budget productions with a series of swashbucklers, Curtiz's history of filming epics in Europe made him the perfect man to direct *Captain Blood, The Adventures of Robin Hood,* and *The Charge of the Light Brigade.*

For all his success on-screen, the director was often considered a terror on the set. A workaholic, Curtiz expected the same of everyone. The first time he worked with Bette Davis, on *Cabin in the Cotton,* he browbeat the young actress mercilessly. Years later, when she complained that he had not called a lunch break, he informed her, "When you work with me, you don't need lunch, just take an aspirin." Errol Flynn became so fed up with his tactics that he finally refused to work with Curtiz. Once, when viewing a marathon dance contest, John Barrymore reportedly turned to his date, who had just marveled at the endurance of the contestants, and quipped, "That's nothing! Have you ever worked for Mike Curtiz?"

During the filming of CASABLANCA, Curtiz (right) predicted Ingrid Bergman's success as Ilsa and advised her to keep playing characters of that type, roles he felt came closest to representing Bergman's true self and, for that reason, would appeal to the filmgoing public.

FOLLOWING OVERLEAF: When it came to framing an image for the screen, Michael Curtiz (right) was one of Hollywood's best.

His methods ultimately endeared him to Jack Warner. Curtiz was always the first to arrive in the morning and the last to go home at night, and he often spent lunch hours pacing around, waiting for the cast and crew to return (that is, when he was not bedding some hopeful young starlet, which he did on a regular basis).

And as hard as he was on his actors, he knew talent when he saw it and knew how to develop it. After putting Bette Davis through a trial by fire on their first film together, he treated her with tremendous respect thereafter. Curtiz had to be forced to cast the untried Errol Flynn as a corpse in the Perry Mason mystery *The Case of the Curious Bride.* But the following year, when British star Robert Donat was forced to withdraw from *Captain Blood,* it was Curtiz who remembered the handsome young actor who had played dead for him.

During the forties, Curtiz continued to demonstrate his value to the studio. He directed one of Flynn's biggest adventures, *The Sea Hawk,* as well as *Yankee Doodle Dandy,* the musical smash that won James Cagney a Best Actor Oscar. He also broke in the studio's new fog machines and created a surprise hit with an adaptation of Jack London's *Wolf Larsen. The Sea Wolf* was a film that embodied the Curtiz touch with its dramatic use of light and shadow to create mood, its skillful combination of heady philosophizing with an action plot, and a strong love story combining cynicism with a sense of impending loss—all elements of *Casablanca.*

Wallis originally wanted James Wong Howe to shoot *Casablanca.* But the photographer was tied up on *The Hard Way,* and no amount of persuasion could get production manager Tenny Wright to release Howe. Wright suggested two other Warners mainstays, Tony Gaudio and Sol Polito, but neither seemed right to Wallis. Finally, the producer settled on Arthur Edeson, a man who

Perc Westmore was the "star" of
the Warner Bros. Makeup Department, helping shape the on-screen
images of all the studio's top
stars. He's shown working on
Olivia de Havilland (left.)

would know how to capture the mystery and intrigue of life in Casablanca.

Edeson, who began his career shooting portraits in his native New York, started as a camera operator in 1911. By the middle of that decade he had become a director of photography in his own right and was one of the founders of the American Society of Cinematographers.

Edeson's first major successes were with such Douglas Fairbanks swashbucklers as *Robin Hood* and *The Thief of Bagdad*, but he would not make a major impact on the industry until 1929, when he shot *In Old Arizona*, the first talking feature filmed on location. He then moved into a comfortable berth at Universal, where he shot another pioneering sound film, *All Quiet on the Western Front*. He also worked on some of director James Whale's best horror films, including *Frankenstein*, *The Old Dark House*, and *The Invisible Man*.

After shooting the Oscar-winning epic *Mutiny on the Bounty* for MGM, Edeson moved to Warner Bros., where he worked on *They Won't Believe Me*, with Claude Rains, and *Each Dawn I Die*, with James Cagney. He also did two films with John Huston, *The Maltese Falcon* and *Across the Pacific*.

Helping Edeson was another Hollywood pioneer, makeup artist Perc ("Pronouced 'purse,'" he always said. "'Perk' is what you do to coffee.") Westmore, who entered the field in 1921 when he created half a moustache for Adolphe Menjou after the actor slipped while shaving and accidentally eliminated 50 percent of his screen

ABOVE: When Orry-Kelly (right) arrived at Warner Bros. in the early 1930s, he brought the studio's stars a sense of style that influenced fashion at the other studios and around the country. His ability to help demanding stars like Bette Davis, Ruth Chatterton, and Kay Francis (left) look their best made him a key player in the Warner Bros. success story. BELOW: The simple look Kelly created for Ingrid Bergman as Ilsa.

trademark. On *Casablanca*, Westmore would have a special challenge—helping Ingrid Bergman look her best without glamorizing her or sacrificing the natural look that had made her a star.

Faced with the same dilemma was Orry-Kelly (his real name except for the hyphen, which was added by studio publicists), the Australian fashion designer who helped revolutionize the Warners Costume Department. Kelly was an established couturier when he arrived on the lot in 1931, becoming one of the first designers to make the transition from high fashion to the silver screen. In fact, he would maintain his own line through much of his fourteen years at Warners, a bone of contention between him and the studio management. When the company tried to capitalize on his work by issuing Studio Styles, a line of dresses adapted from his film designs, he refused to allow them to use his name. Instead, each item bore a label reading "Designed by Warner Bros. Ace Designer."

PREVIOUS OVERLEAF: The only CASABLANCA scene filmed off the Warner Bros. lot was the arrival of Major Strasser's plane, shot at the Los Angeles Municipal Airport.

BELOW: Score for CASABLANCA's title music, by Max Steiner (opposite), one of the chief composers on the Warners lot. The orchestrations were done by Hugo Friedhofer, later an acclaimed film composer in his own right.

R ounding out the list of film pioneers assigned to *Casablanca* was Max Steiner, who almost single-handedly defined the way films were scored in the early days of sound. Steiner was born in Vienna, where he displayed his prodigious talents early. He completed the eight-year course at Vienna's Imperial Academy of Music in one, graduating at age thirteen. His first project after leaving the academy was the score for a musical that ran for two years. He then studied composition with Gustave Mahler and made his symphonic conducting debut at the age of sixteen.

In 1914, the twenty-six-year-old Steiner emigrated to America to escape the ravages of World War I. For the next decade and a half, he was a mainstay of the Broadway musical, both as an orchestrator and conductor for such luminaries as Victor Herbert and Flo Ziegfeld. With the coming of talking pictures, Steiner saw a new outlet for his talents. Although live orchestral accompaniment had been a key part of the presentation of silent films, most early talking pictures had little or no music. Many people in the industry thought that background music would confuse the audience, making them wonder where the sound was coming from.

Steiner, however, saw that background music could play an important role in driving the audience's emotions. He signed on with RKO Pictures in 1929 and, with the help of David O. Selznick, who ran the studio from 1931 to 1933, created a series of scores whose melodic richness and thematic unity actually helped sell tickets. The most notable of his early achievements there were the scores for the South Seas romance *Bird of Paradise* and for one of the most popular pictures ever made, *King Kong*.

After winning his first Oscar, for John Ford's *The Informer*, Steiner moved to Warner Bros., the studio with which he would be

most closely identified. In fact, he even composed the Warner Bros. fanfare, which would introduce every one of the studio's films (except those scored by Erich Wolfgang Korngold) from 1936 on.

At Warners, Steiner's most notable scores were the ones he wrote for Bette Davis's pictures, including *Jezebel*, with its lilting nineteenth-century waltz; *Dark Victory*, with heavenly choirs singing Davis to death in the final reel; and *Now, Voyager*, where his creative use of the theme song he wrote for Davis and Paul Henreid, "It Can't Be Wrong," brought him his second Oscar.

The most famous of Steiner's more than two hundred scores was written not at Warners, but on loan-out to his original Hollywood mentor, Selznick. The title theme Steiner composed for *Gone With the Wind*

CASABLANCA's art director, Carl Jules Weyl, is pictured second row, center. Hal Wallis (opposite, bottom left), Humphrey Bogart, and Michael Curtiz confer with Lieutenant Robert Aisner (in uniform), the film's technical adviser, on the set for the Paris train station.

is one of the two most recognizable pieces of music from the Golden Age of Hollywood. The other, of course, is "As Time Goes By" from *Casablanca*, a song Steiner did not write, but one he wove skillfully throughout the score.

The cutting of *Casablanca* was entrusted to Owen Marks, who had been a mainstay of the Warners Editing Department since the days of silent films, working on everything from *Disraeli* to *The Private Lives of Elizabeth and Essex*. Carl Jules Weyl, the art director who had created the Malaysian backdrop for *The Letter* and the small-town splendor of *Kings Row*, was charged with turning parts of the Culver City backlot into French Morocco. Don Siegel, who learned how to tell a story cinematically as a member of the inserts department before moving on to a distinguished directing career with films like *Invasion of the Body Snatchers* and *Dirty Harry*, would create the opening montage. And for technical advisor, Curtiz found a French army officer, Lieutenant Robert Aisner, who not only had escaped from a German concentration camp, but had traveled through Casablanca on his own trek along the refugee trail.

The people were in place. They were all pointed in the same general direction. But as of May 25, 1942—with no final script approved—they were not exactly sure yet what their final destination would be.

34 Countries 34

Warners' PR Department proudly hailed *Casablanca* for involving thirty-four different nationalities. It is hard to find all of them—and the publicists were not above inventing a foreign birthplace where it fit their needs—but here is a brief list of some of the different countries represented on- and off-screen in *Casablanca*:

Australia ....Costume designer Orry-Kelly

Austria ....Paul Henreid, Helmut Dantine, Ludwig Stossel, composer Max Steiner

Canada ....John Qualen

China ....Madam Nellie Chiang

England...........Claude Rains, Sydney Greenstreet, prop man Limey Plews

France ....Madeleine Le Beau, Marcel Dalio, technical advisor Lieutenant Robert Aisner

Germany..........Conrad Veidt, Curt Bois, Trudy Berliner

Hungary ....Peter Lorre, S. Z. Sakall, Michael Curtiz

Italy...............Frank Puglia

Russia ....Leonid Kinsky, Dina Smirnova

Sweden ....Ingrid Bergman

Turkey ....Abdullah Kareem

United States ...Humphrey Bogart, Dooley Wilson, Joy Page, Corinna Mura, Dan Seymour, Hal Wallis, Julius and Philip Epstein, Howard Koch, cinematographer Arthur Edeson.

Chapter Four

It's Still A
STORY
Without An
ENDING

As casting and other assignments for *Casablanca* moved along, the writing began to fall behind. The first set of script pages from the Epsteins had elicited a variety of responses. Curtiz felt that the role of Strasser was too weak and suggested making the character older and upgrading him from captain to major so he could be more of an antagonist, thus clarifying the script's conflict. That was easy enough.

What required more work was the character of Rick. Reportedly, Bogart got one look at the script and complained that the character had no background and less backbone. All Rick did was sit around and whine. To help capture a stronger sense of the story's political issues, Howard Koch was assigned to the script on April 6, 1942. Few of those involved in the creation of Warner Bros. Production No. 410 got to *Casablanca* by as long and circuitous a route as Koch. His journey started on New York's East Side, where he was born in 1902. When his father got a job with the New York Board of Water Supply, the family moved to a small town in upstate New York, where Koch was more readily accepted by his schoolmates than his Jewish mother and father were by their neighbors.

The next step for Koch was college, which the gifted young scholar entered at the age of sixteen. The socially conscious Koch was determined to become a lawyer. He got his degree at Columbia, but was soon disillusioned with the legal profession. To escape, he began going to the theater. Intrigued by the workings of the many plays he had enjoyed, Koch bought a copy of George S. Kaufman's *The Butter and Egg Man*. Before long, he had written a play of his own, *He Went to College*, a comedy about an eager young radical bringing his politics home to his parents. He even won a short Broadway production.

For his next piece, he tried a more serious family problem play called *Give Us This Day*. This, too, got into production, but as rehearsals proceeded, Koch became aware that someone else was rewriting the script for him (a situation not unlike what he would face during the filming of *Casablanca*). When the altered play opened to poor reviews in New York, the fledgling playwright was actually relieved.

Koch's next play was *The Lonely Man*, a fantasy in which Abraham Lincoln came back to Earth in the 1930s only to discover that slavery still existed, but the chains were economic rather than physical. John Huston was so successful playing Lincoln that the play lasted an entire season in Chicago. And that success was important to Koch. Huston would eventually wind up in Hollywood, where he would be instrumental in furthering the young writer's career. Also, the script attracted the attention of John Houseman of the Mercury Theatre. The company was branching out into radio with CBS's "The Mercury Theatre of the Air," produced, directed, starring, and written by (at least in the credits) Orson Welles. As Welles's assistant, Houseman was charged with finding someone skillful, hardy, and foolish enough to take

OPPOSITE: Howard Koch accepts the Academy Award for Best Screenplay for CASABLANCA. The award also went to Julius J. and Philip G. Epstein, the other two writers credited with the script. Not mentioned were Aeneas McKenzie and Wally Kline, who did the original adaptation; Casey Robinson, who made major contributions to the romantic scenes and suggested making the leading lady European; and Lenore Coffee, who also worked on the romantic element. BELOW: Michael Curtiz accepts his Oscar for Best Director; "Daily Worker" story on 1943 Oscars.

'Casablanca' Wins 1943 Award 'Oscar'

Newspaper article on public reaction to "The War of the Worlds." The Orson Welles production made Howard Koch a hot property in Hollywood. Years later, he would describe the experience in his book THE PANIC BROADCAST: PORTRAIT OF AN EVENT.

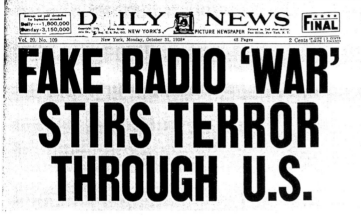

DAILY NEWS FINAL

Average net paid circulation for September amounted to
Daily---1,800,000
Sunday-3,150,000

NEW YORK'S PICTURE NEWSPAPER

Vol. 20. No. 109   New York, Monday, October 31, 1938*   48 Pages   2 Cents

FAKE RADIO 'WAR' STIRS TERROR THROUGH U.S.

New York World-Telegram

AND THE EVENING MAIL

A SCRIPPS-HOWARD NEWSPAPER.

ROY W. HOWARD, President and Editor; LEE B. WOOD, Executive Editor; MERLIN H. AYLESWORTH, Publisher; N. S. MACNEISH, Business Manager.

Phone BArclay 7-3211.

Owned and published daily (except Sunday) by New York World-Telegram Corporation. Main office 125 Barclay Street. Branch office 147 West 42nd Street, corner Broadway (Room 204).

Member of United Press Associated Press. Scripps-Howard Newspaper Alliance NEA Service, Inc.; Newspaper Information Service, which organizations retain exclusive rights to all news and features credited to them. Member of the Audit Bureau of Circulations. The Associated Press is exclusively entitled to the use for republication of all news dispatches credited to it or not otherwise credited in this paper

SCRIPPS-HOWARD

"Give Light and the People Will Find Their Own Way."

Subscription rate by mail for New York World-Telegram in the United States (outside of New York City), one year, $12.00.

TUESDAY, NOVEMBER 1, 1938.

"Frighted with False Fire."

It is strange and disturbing that thousands of Americans, secure in their homes on a quiet Sunday evening, could be scared out of their wits by a radio dramatization of H. G. Wells' fantastic old story, "The War of the Worlds."

We're sure the 23-year-old actor, Orson Welles, didn't realize the panic he was spreading from coast to coast among people who believed that monsters from Mars actually had invaded New Jersey.

Yet young Mr. Welles, a student of Shakespeare, might have remembered Hamlet and, remembering, might have foreseen the effect of too much dramatic realism on an audience already strung to high nervous tension.

Hamlet it was who staged a play to "catch the conscience" of the King of Denmark, his uncle, who had murdered Hamlet's father, seized the throne and married the widowed queen. This play within a play also concerned the murder of a king. And, as Hamlet had intended, his uncle and his mother were driven to such hysterical terror that they refused to watch it to the end.

"What, frighted with false fire!" exclaimed Hamlet with bitter scorn, certain now of his uncle's guilt.

Unlike Hamlet, young Mr. Welles did not plan deliberately to demoralize his audience. And no guilty consciences, but nerves made jittery by actual, though almost incredible, threats of war and disaster, had prepared a good many American radio listeners to believe the completely incredible "news" that Martian hordes were here.

Of course it should never happen again. But we don't agree with those who are arguing that the Sunday night scare shows a need for strict government censorship of radio programs.

On the contrary, we think it is evidence of how dangerous political control of radio might become. If so many people could be misled unintentionally, when the purpose was merely to entertain, what could designing politicians not do through control of broadcasting stations.

The dictators in Europe use radio to make their people believe falsehoods. We want nothing like that here. Better have American radio remain free to make occasional blunders than start on a course that might, in time, deprive it of freedom to broadcast uncensored truth.

And it should be easy for radio to avoid repeating this particular blunder. The Columbia system, as a result of its unhappy experience Sunday night, has already pointed the way. Let all chains, all stations, avoid use of the news broadcasting technique in dramatizations when there is any possibility of any listener mistaking fiction for fact.

---

on the task of writing one hour-long radio drama per week. He found Howard Koch.

For two weeks, Koch worked almost non-stop writing and rewriting to order for Welles and Houseman. His third assignment was an adaptation of H.G. Wells's *The War of the Worlds*. Welles wanted the story told in the first person and presented as a series of news broadcasts. Over the next six days, Koch gleefully set his Martians to destroying many of New York's greatest landmarks, including CBS headquarters. But when the play was presented on October 30, 1938, people missed the joke. Instead, large portions of the radio audience thought they were listening to actual news reports of a Martian invasion, and the nation was thrown into a panic.

Nothing else in Koch's career would equal the notoriety of this broadcast. With a script credit for the most famous hour of radio ever, Koch was a hot property. With John Huston's help, he landed a writing position at Warner Bros.

For weeks, Koch was without an assignment, a situation Huston blamed on typecasting, joking that Koch would be given a script as soon as the studio came up with a story about Martians. Finally, Koch was asked to help Robert Buckner with the script for *Virginia City*. Then he was sent the treatment for a new screen version of Rafael Sabatini's *The Sea Hawk*. Koch did the unthinkable for a young writer in Hollywood: he turned the assignment down.

When producer Henry Blanke asked why Koch did not want to do the script, the writer identified the problems with the story so eloquently that he was told to go ahead and try the script his own way. The result was one of Errol Flynn's best films, a period swashbuckler with strong parallels to the political situation in Europe.

Koch's next assignment was Warners' prestige picture for 1940, *The Letter*, an adaptation of W. Somerset Maugham's play to star Bette Davis under William Wyler's direction. That project was followed by a collaboration with

John Huston on the life story of World War I's most decorated soldier, *Sergeant York*, and Huston's second film as a director, a mangled translation of Ellen Glasgow's Pulitzer Prize-winning *In This Our Life*.

After being assigned to *Casablanca* on April 6, Koch worked with the Epsteins for two weeks, then was left pretty much on his own. He also began meeting informally with Bogart in the star's dressing room. Over drinks, they discussed a variety of subjects, but invariably the conversation returned to *Casablanca*.

Koch was under a tight deadline. Production had to start by May 25 so that Bogart could honor a loan-out to Columbia Pictures, where he would film *Sahara* later in the summer. Veidt and Wilson needed to report for other films at MGM and Paramount, respectively. On the front end of the schedule, Henreid, Rains, and Greenstreet were all involved in films with which they had to be finished in time for *Casablanca* to start. And Bogart had requested as much vacation time as possible following *Across the Pacific*, the film he was just finishing up.

The next set of script pages, a revision of Part I, was submitted May 11. As already decided, the role of Strasser had been beefed up, and his initial confrontation with Victor is in the form it will take in the finished film. In addition, with Bergman now cast, the leading lady has become the decidedly more sympathetic Ilsa.

Rick, also, is a stronger character and, thanks to Koch, has more of a political background than he had in the play or in the script's first draft. The first indication of this is the incident in which Rick turns a patron away from the gambling room. No longer is the rejected customer an Englishman with a history of writing bad checks. He is now a German, and there is no reason given for Rick's

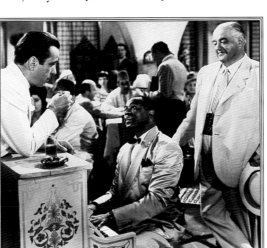

Señor Ferrari offers to buy Sam's contract from Rick, a scene from the original play that the screenwriters (possibly Howard Koch) gave a political spin by adding Rick's line, "I don't buy or sell human beings."

refusal to do business with him—just a cryptic exchange that could indicate Rick's behavior is more politically motivated than even he would like to admit:

RICK: Your cash is good at the bar.
GERMAN: Do you know who I am?
RICK: I do. You're lucky the bar's open to you.

Rick's scene with Martinez (later Ferrari) also takes on a more political tinge. This time, when the rival café owner offers to buy Sam's contract, Rick replies, "I don't buy or sell human beings," setting up the respectful nature of his relationship with the black man.

The political aspect of Rick's past is decidedly more explicit. Gone for good are the wife and children left behind in *Everybody Comes to Rick's*. In their place is a history as a patron saint of lost causes. Renault now confronts Rick specifically about his past deeds:

RENAULT: ...my dear Ricky, I suspect that under that cynical shell you're at heart a sentimentalist....Oh, laugh if you will, but I happen to be familiar with your record. Let me point out just two items. In 1935 you ran guns to Ethiopia. In 1936, you fought in Spain on the Loyalists' side.
RICK: And got well paid for it on both occasions.
RENAULT: The winning side would have paid you much better.

This draft runs through the Paris flashback, where there is another reference to Rick's political involvement. When he and Ilsa hear news of the Nazis' approach, they know it is time for him to get out of town:

RICK: Nothing can stop them now. Wednesday, Thursday at the latest, they'll be in Paris.

ILSA: *(Frightened)* Richard, they'll find out your record. It won't be safe for you here.

RICK: *(Smiles)* I'm on their blacklist already, their roll of honor.

One curiosity about this draft is the handling of Rick and Ilsa's reunion. In this version, Ilsa does not have to encourage Sam to play "As Time Goes By." She does not even request it. He just plays it for old time's sake. When Rick approaches the table, Ilsa is alone, paving the way for a much franker confrontation between the two. In fact, their scene—complete with Ilsa's explanation of why she left Rick in Paris and Rick's cynical, conversation-ending, "Tell me, who was it you left me for? Was it Laszlo, or were there others in between? Or aren't you the kind that tells?"—is almost identical to the scene Rick and Ilsa will play in the finished film when she returns to the café after closing.

At this point in the writing process, Wallis sent Howard Koch a memo asking him to speed up his work as much as possible and finish the screenplay "within the next two or three days if you can." Koch's immediate reply gives some idea of his problems with the script. Although he notes that the Epsteins follow the new plot (presumably the transformation of Lois into Ilsa and the changes in Strasser's role), the tone of their work is decidedly different from what Koch had been asked to write: "They apparently see the situations more in terms of their comic possibilities, while my effort has been to legitimize the characters and develop a serious melodrama of present-day significance, using humor merely as a relief from dramatic tension." In essence, Koch felt he was taking what was most usable from the Epsteins' submissions and creating an entirely new screenplay. That was a process he could not rush without a loss of quality.

A week later, Koch had finished the second third of the script. Structurally, the story has been opened up considerably, with scenes in Strasser's and Renault's offices, the bazaar, and Martinez's club, the Blue Parrot. In fact, there are relatively few differences between this draft and the *Casablanca* we know. One of those differences is the scene in which Ilsa meets Rick in the bazaar. In an exchange that echoes the depiction of Lois in the original play, she tries to appear as heartless as he has made her out to be:

ILSA: You had to leave Paris. I didn't. If I went with you, I thought of what it would be like—cheap hotels, hiding from the police, no purpose, no destination—just running away.

RICK: And you didn't love me enough for that.

ILSA: No, Rick, not quite enough.

RICK: Well, I'm not running now. I'm settled down—above a saloon, it's true, but— *(ironically)* Walk up a flight. You'll find it worth your while.

ILSA: No, thanks. We had our red-letter days together in Paris. That was enough for a lifetime.

The bazaar scene also contains a new element in her background. This is the first draft in which the leading lady is married to Victor.

Also of note is a change in the depiction of Renault's character. In this draft, Renault is much more clearly caught in the middle between the Third Reich on one side and Rick and the Laszlos on the other. In the first scene after the Paris flashback, Strasser and Renault discuss Rick's connection to Ugarte:

STRASSER: I strongly suspect that Ugarte left the letters of transit with Mr. Blaine. I would suggest you search the cafe immediately and thoroughly.

RENAULT: If Rick has the letters, he's much too smart to let you find them there.

STRASSER: You give him credit for too much cleverness. My impression was that he's just another blundering American.

RENAULT: But we mustn't underestimate American blundering. *(Innocently)* I was with them when they "blundered" into Berlin in 1918.

This confrontation puts Renault's position in a new light. Koch has written that, for him, the dramatic center of the film was less the romance between Rick and Ilsa than the friendly verbal sparring between Rick and Renault. In line with his assignment to get

In the Black Market, Rick and Ilsa argue about their past. Ilsa's revelation that she is married to Victor would solve one censorship problem (the objection to what seemed to be an illicit affair between the two traveling companions) and create another (the fact that Ilsa was married to Victor during her affair with Rick).

a stronger sense of politics into the film, he concentrated on the way events pushed Rick and Renault into involvement with the Allied cause.

From this point, it becomes virtually impossible to determine who wrote what. Subsequent drafts bear no writer credit, and even the participants are not really sure what they contributed beyond some key elements that would naturally stand out in the memory. Concerned over the current draft's lack of attention to the film's romantic elements, Wallis sent his friend Casey Robinson a copy—including scenes from the last third of the film—with a request for his comments. On May 20 Robinson replied, supporting what Wallis feared, the melodrama and humor were working fine, but the romantic element was "deficient."

He made some very definite suggestions about the development of the love story. It was Robinson's idea to move the first private meeting between Rick and Ilsa to later in the evening, after the café has closed for the night.

The second scene Robinson suggested would have taken place in Rick's apartment the following afternoon. It is here that Robinson would have Ilsa explain the real reason she left Rick in Paris, her marriage to Laszlo. At the same time, her description of her love for Victor—"her admiration, respect, even veneration. To her, [Victor] is the personification of the best ideals of her nature, of honor, of sacrifice for a great cause"—begins to win Rick over.

Next, according to Robinson, should come the scene in which Laszlo asks for Rick's help. Now, Rick is not so certain of Ilsa's character any more. "He suspects he has been played for a sucker, and if there is anything Rick doesn't like to be, it's a sucker." This would lead logically to a line that apparently had already been written: Rick refuses to help Laszlo and, when asked for a reason, responds, "Ask your wife."

Finally, Robinson comes to the big confrontation between Rick and Ilsa: "I would play the beginning of the next scene between Rick and Ilsa pretty much as it is, but greatly alter the finish. Ilsa comes for the visas. She tries to be hard-boiled. She can't be. She breaks down completely. But completely. She tells Rick that she loves him and will do anything he wants. She will go anywhere, stay here, anything. She is absolutely helpless in the great passionate love she has for him. She will leave Victor. Rick can get him out of Casablanca. She knows that she's doing wrong, she even says so. She knows that in a way it is a violation of all the high idealism and honor of her nature. She knows she

is being wicked but she can't help herself. This is a great scene for a woman to play.

"At the end of the scene, she says that she will go home to her husband and tell him. With an enigmatic look on his face, Rick tells her not to do it. Better that she come with her husband to his place for the letters without telling her husband first, for otherwise he might not come. Better, anyway, that they tell him together.

"Now you're really set up for a swell twist when Rick sends her away on the plane with Victor. For now, in doing so, he is not just solving a love triangle. He is forcing the girl to live up to the idealism of her nature, forcing her to carry on with the work that in these days is far more important than the love of two little peo-

BELOW: Casey Robinson (right) and Fredric March (left) on the set of ONE FOOT IN HEAVEN. OPPOSITE: Before Victor arrives at the café to pick up the exit visas, Rick tells Ilsa they will explain their plans to him later at the airport, prophetically adding, "The less time to think, the easier for all of us."

ple. It is something they will both be glad for when the pain is over...."

With the exception of his idea for the afternoon scene between Rick and Ilsa set in Rick's apartment, all of Robinson's suggestions would wind up in the film.

Another key player in adjusting the *Casablanca* screenplay was Joseph I. Breen, head of the Motion Picture Producers and Distributors Association (MPPDA) and administrator of the industry's production code. The MPPDA found two areas of the *Casablanca* screenplay "unacceptably sex suggestive": the depiction of Renault's sexual escapades and the treatment of Rick and Ilsa's relationship.

In dealing with Renault, suggestions from the Breen office often seem ludicrous. When Renault enters as Rick is sending Yvonne off, his line, "How extravagant you are—throwing away women like that. Some day they may be

rationed," had to be changed so that it ended with, "Some day they may be scarce." Later, Renault's comment that Rick's work at least "keeps you out of doors" had to be changed to "gets you plenty of fresh air," lest the audience draw its own conclusions about the nature of Renault's indoor labors. Judged totally unacceptable was an exchange in which Renault is informed that "another visa problem has come up" and responds, "Show her in."

In the matter of the love story, however, at least one of Breen's suggestions would actually improve the picture. Wallis had already deleted the play's most censorable element, Lois's return to the café to sleep with Rick in order to get the exit visas. The decision to have Ilsa leave Rick in Paris because of her marriage to Victor raised other problems, however. The MPPDA could not approve the suggestion that Ilsa had had an affair with Rick in Paris while she was already married to Victor. In a compromise, Ilsa revealed that at the time she met Rick she thought Victor was dead. His return, just as she was preparing to leave Paris, actually gave her a stronger reason for deserting Rick and made the story of their impossible love more compelling.

Even here, however, the Breen office carried its role as watchdog to almost ridiculous extremes. In June, after reading the latest version of the scene in Rick's Casablanca apartment—in which Ilsa starts out to get the exit visas, then admits she loves Rick—Breen insisted that there be no indication whatsoever that the two made love. As written, there is a time shift in the middle of the scene. The action ends with her declaration of love and resumes as she is telling Rick why she originally left him. In a letter dated June 18, 1942, Breen writes: "The present material seems to contain a suggestion of a sex affair which would be unacceptable if it came through in the finished picture. We believe this could possibly be corrected by replacing the fade out on page 135, with a dissolve, and shooting the succeeding scene without any sign of a bed or couch,

Samba Casablanca

Rick finally got Ilsa, though it took him forty-five years to do so. Brazilian film fan Joao Luiz Albuquerque took a print of the film apart and reassembled it to suit his tastes, complete with an ending in which Ilsa did not get on the plane with Victor. This unauthorized, re-edited version of the film, given a special, private showing at the Rio Film Festival in 1987, also bore one of the more unusual credits in cinema history: "Copyright infringements by Joao Luiz Albuquerque."

or anything whatever suggestive of a sex affair."

All of this emphasis on sexuality should not obscure another important role played by the MPPDA. In reviewing scripts and finished films, the organization also advised the studios on the likely impact of their treatment of characters from other countries. With *Casablanca*, the MPPDA advised making it clear that the singer at Rick's Café is a South American since the character was sympathetic and, as such, would play well with U.S. allies south of the border. In the same light, the studio was advised to make it clear that such negative characters as Ugarte, Martinez, and the Dark European were not from any allied or neutral country. This probably accounts for the late name change of Martinez to the more Italian Ferrari.

As these suggestions were coming in, Koch was working feverishly to finish the script before the film's May 25 start date. He made it four days early. On May 21, the final third of the script was distributed. As before, much of the action is similar to the final film. In this version, Rick helps Jan win at roulette so the young Bulgarian couple can get out of Casablanca with Mrs. Viereck's honor intact. Rick refuses to give Victor the exit visas, but later nods his approval for the band to play "*La Marseillaise.*" And Ilsa comes to Rick's apartment to force him to hand over the letters of transit, only to give in to her love for him.

In the apartment scene, there is a pronounced difference from the finished film. In this draft, there is no resistance meeting for Victor to attend, so he cannot show up at the café just in time to, unknowingly, prevent Rick and Ilsa from going to bed together. Instead, there's a clear indication that the lovers did more than talk:

RICK: Stop thinking about Victor.
ILSA: I can't. I can't be that callous—
RICK: I can. I'm in love. I'm the one who really needs you. He's got work, a Cause. He's in love with People, but I'm in love with you.

Rick tries to get his rejected lover Yvonne (Madeleine Le Beau) to leave quietly. Their relationship is one of the most sexually explicit in the film. Even here, however, the MPPDA made some demands for cuts, particularly when Renault chides Rick for tossing Yvonne aside, saying, "Some day they [women] may be rationed."

ILSA: *(Looks at him with tear-dimmed eyes. In a whisper)* I wish you weren't. I wish I weren't in love with you. *(He takes her in his arms and kisses her. It is a long kiss. When they finally disengage, Ilsa looks up at him. Tenderly)* We're still terrible people. *(They kiss again)*
FADE OUT

The finale is also different from what would ultimately be filmed. Rick acts as though he were betraying Victor, telling Renault to come by the café and catch the resistance leader with the stolen exit visas. But as in both play and film, Rick turns the tables on Renault, pulling a gun on him. The rest of the film plays out in the café. Rick informs Ilsa that he is sending her off with Victor, but not with any lines contemporary audiences would recognize:

RICK: Do you think I'm going to let you rot here? I can never get out. I've got no place to go and nothing to do when I get there—

ILSA: I don't care, Rick. I don't care—

RICK: I'm not the Rick you knew in Paris. I'm not a man you can love anymore. I serve drinks. I run a crooked gambling table. Every morning I lock myself in a room and drink myself dizzy.

Rick turns the tables on Renault, setting the stage for the film's conclusion—but what that conclusion would be was not settled until just before it was filmed. In Koch's initial treatment of the scene, only Victor and Ilsa make it to the airport. Rick holds Renault at gunpoint in the café, which also serves as the setting for Rick's final confrontation with Strasser.

That's all I'll be doing every day and night for the rest of my life—

ILSA: Then I'll do it with you.

RICK: No, I've got it down to a science now. I don't need any help doing it. I don't want you around. *(Pointing to Laszlo)* You go with him. He wants you. I'm all finished. You belong to a fighter, not a saloon-keeper.

ILSA: *(Tearfully)* If you think you can talk me out of it—

But before she can say any more, Renault interrupts by stating that Rick will be spending the rest of his days in a concentration camp.

With that, Victor and Ilsa leave. Strasser arrives, and he and Rick fight, with the Ger-

man winning. Before he can get to the phone and order his men to stop the Laszlos, however, Rick gets the gun and shoots him.

What was to happen next was a major problem. Wallis did not just discuss the matter with Michael Curtiz and Howard Koch, he also called back the Epsteins to get their ideas. The play's ending, with Rick sent off to prison for helping the Laszlos, was unacceptable by Hollywood standards. His heroism deserved some kind of reward, even if he had not gotten the girl.

It was the Epsteins who came up with the solution. As Julius Epstein told Ronald Haver for an article in *American Film*, the twins were driving home one night when they suddenly turned to each other and said simultaneously, "Round up the usual suspects." The line, building on one they had written for Renault earlier, would allow them to get Rick off the hook and also provide a fitting conclusion for the relationship they and Koch had developed for Rick and Renault.

To conclude the script, Rick responded to Renault's sudden show of generosity in a cynical manner also characteristic of their relationship, "It doesn't make a bit of difference, Louis. You still owe me five thousand francs."

So as of May 21, 1942, the script for *Casablanca* was done—but far from finished. Even though shooting was only four days away, nobody thought of this as the final draft. It was simply an outline that would allow production to finalize the budget, schedule the shoot, and know what props, costumes, sets, actors, etc., would be needed. In addition, as hard as Howard Koch had worked and as effective as his work had been at adding a stronger political subtext to the plot, Hal Wallis and Michael Curtiz were still not totally satisfied with his script pages, particularly in his handling of the story's romantic side. As Wallis indicated in a memo to production manager Tenny Wright, there would still be changes. He had also calculated that any delays caused by

"Major Strasser's been shot. Round up the usual suspects." By May 21, 1942, the Epsteins had figured out how to get Rick off the hook for killing the Nazi commander. It wasn't until a later draft, however, that the shooting would be moved from Rick's Café to the Casablanca airport.

the lack of a suitable script would cost Warner Bros. $30,000 per day. So, Wallis and Curtiz gave up their Sundays for meetings with one or another of the writers. They would assemble at Curtiz's ranch and go over ideas, trying to figure out what words they would be filming in the week ahead.

All of this confusion in settling on a final script has given rise to one of the most widely believed myths about *Casablanca*: that the film was shot in sequence because the last pages of the script had not yet been written. This is not borne out by the production reports. Each day, production manager Al Alleborn would fill out a form stating what hours the company worked, what actors appeared in scenes, what scenes were shot, and what sets were used. According to these production reports, *Casablanca* was shot in pieces as sets and people became available, just like any other film.

Casablanca had to be scheduled around other productions on the Warners lot. The film's largest set, Rick's Café, took up all of Soundstage 8 and included countless props and furniture pieces, some of them Warners' stock,

To cut costs, art director Carl Jules Weyl transformed the New England train station from NOW, VOYAGER (above) into the Paris train station (left) where Rick discovers Ilsa has deserted him. The company would have to wait until June 3, 1942, to film on the set. BELOW: The "swank Paris café" where Rick and Ilsa dance during the flashback.

others on loan. To have shot the film in sequence would have meant keeping the soundstage and all of the materials involved tied up for weeks while scenes were filmed on other sets. No Hollywood studio could have afforded to operate like that. Therefore, quite naturally, all of the scenes at Rick's Café were shot over the course of six weeks, with a few days on other sets as they became available.

Three sets to be used in *Casablanca* had actually been created for other films. The Paris railroad station, where Rick learns that Ilsa has left him, was actually the New England railroad station built for *Now, Voyager*. Señor Ferrari's café, the Blue Parrot, and the Black Market were sets from *The Desert Song*, which was shooting at the same time. In using these, the company would have to work around the schedules for the other movies.

In addition to set problems, filming revolved around the actors' schedules. It was rare indeed for every member of a film's cast to be totally available throughout shooting. On *Casablanca*, production would be slowed down while the company waited for Paul Henreid and Claude Rains to finish *Now, Voyager*; for Curt Bois to finish *Princess O'Rourke*; and for Sydney Greenstreet to finish *Background to Danger*.

"CASA BLANCA"
CURTIZ CO. 410-10
STAGE 14 LOCATION
SET STILL INT-
RICKS APT.
DATE

"CASA BLANCA"
CURTIZ CO. 410-06
STAGE 14 LOCATION
SET STILL INT.
ILSA'S APT.

The sets for Rick's and Ilsa's Paris apartments (opposite top and opposite bottom) were built specifically for CASABLANCA. The Black Market (left) and Señor Ferrari's Blue Parrot (below), however, were built for THE DESERT SONG, which was filming at the same time. Waiting for these sets to be available would add to the production delays and put Sydney Greenstreet's (Ferrari) salary over budget.

CASABLANCA AÉRO-GARE

A set piece (above) and matte painting (opposite, bottom) were used to transform the Los Angeles Airport into Casablanca for Major Strasser's arrival. Opposite, top, are plans for repainting the plane on which he arrived. It was refurbished in Arizona, then flown to California, though there is no record of any public reaction to the sight of a Nazi plane winging its way over Los Angeles.

Chapter Five

Go Ahead And
SHOOT,
You'll Be Doing Me A
FAVOR

ABOVE: One of many memos Wallis
wrote complaining that the scenes
shot in Rick's Place were too
brightly lit. He began with com-
plaints to Director of Photography
Arthur Edeson, then turned his
attention to Curtiz, who got Edeson
shoot the sets properly. BELOW:
The first scene filmed was set at
La Belle Aurore, the French café
where Rick, Ilsa, and Sam share a
last bottle of champagne before
the Germans arrive. OPPOSITE: Rick
and Ilsa ride an excursion
boat on the Seine during the Paris
flashback in a scene shot on the
third day of filming.

The first piece of the *Casablanca* jigsaw puzzle was put into place on May 25, 1942, when shooting began with the Paris flashback scenes. Although the flashback does not occur until approximately one-third of the way into the script, it was a good place to start. The scene only involved three of the principle actors—Humphrey Bogart, Ingrid Bergman, and Dooley Wilson—making it possible to work around roles not cast or actors who were not yet available. The flashbacks could be done on smaller sets while the studio's carpenters were completing Rick's Café. And finally, it was a perfect choice for the two stars, giving them the rare luxury of playing out Rick and Ilsa's past before having to play scenes based on their memories of that past.

The first day's shooting was ruined by problems with the sound recording. For some reason, the sound operator had neglected to tell anyone that the overhead lights were emitting an audible hiss that made everything printed that day unusable. Wallis had to explain the problem to the actors personally and assure them that everything was really going very well.

There also were problems with the lighting. According to a memo from Wallis, Director of Photography Arthur Edeson took so long lighting the sets that there was no time to get through all the scheduled scenes. The Montmartre café scenes had to be put off to another day. Wallis wrote: "I, too, want a beautiful photographic job on this picture, which offers a great deal of background and color for a cameraman, but you were present at all the meetings we had about all the war emergencies and the necessity of conserving money and material, and I must ask you to sacrifice a little on quality, if necessary, in order not to take these long periods of time for setups."

Wallis's biggest problem, though, was with his trusted director. For some reason, Curtiz shot a simple driving scene without recording any of the dialogue. And he omitted another scene from the flashback altogether, even though it had been scheduled. With the other time problems

More scenes from the Paris flash-back: (below) Rick and Ilsa toast each other in her apartment in the first scene in which Rick says, "Here's looking at you, kid"; the street café (bottom) where they discuss Rick's position on the Nazis' "roll of honor."

that would affect the film, these mistakes were never corrected, so in the finished film, Rick and Ilsa drive wordlessly past the Arc de Triomphe.

The irony behind these omissions is that Curtiz had fought to keep the Paris flashback in the film. Howard Koch had not wanted to write the scenes at all, claiming that they slowed the picture down at a crucial point, just after Rick has discovered that Ilsa is in Casablanca. Curtiz had argued successfully that the scenes were necessary to let the audience see the closeness the two lovers had shared in Paris. This disagreement points up the key difference between Koch's and Curtiz's visions of the film. For Koch, the love story was a peg on which to hang a tale of one man's political involvement, and the flashback was just so much romantic filler that kept the picture from getting to the point. To Curtiz, the politics were just background to a tale of two people in love.

The Paris flashback marked the addition of one of *Casablanca*'s most important lines, Rick's catchphrase, "Here's looking at you, kid." In the script issued four days before filming began, the line is, "Here's good luck to you." "Here's looking at you, kid," doesn't turn up in a written script until June 1, a week after the Paris flashback was shot. Some observers have said that the line was suggested by Bogart, who also is credited with changing "Of all the *cafés* in all the cities in all the world, she walks into *my café*," from the May 21 script, to "Of all the *gin joints* in all the cities in all the world, she walks into *mine*."

But if Bogart was helpful in shaping some of Rick's most important utterances, he was not doing much to establish a romantic rapport with Ingrid Bergman between scenes. Bergman was disappointed by his standoffishness. With no other way to get to know him, she screened *The Maltese Falcon* repeatedly so she could come to understand his acting style and get a stronger sense of the screen image with which she was supposed to be in love. Later, she would say of their working relationship, "I kissed him, but I never knew him."

Off-screen, Bogie's behavior was probably not intentionally rude. When he wanted to be rude to a co-star, he was just plain rude. Most often, this took the form of snide comments about the other performer's acting, professionalism, or lack thereof. In fact, two former co-stars, George Raft and Ida Lupino, refused to work with him again because of this.

But his standoffish attitude was in part deliberate. Initially, he had been concerned that Bergman's freshness and talent would wipe him off the screen. One of his advisors, Mel Baker, told him, "This is the first time you've ever played the romantic lead against a major star. You stand still, and always make her come to you. Mike probably won't notice it, and if she complains you can tell her it's tacit in the script. You've got something she wants, so she has to come to you." With that in mind, Bogart found every place possible to make Bergman come to him, with the result that audiences believed he held some magnetic power over her.

There was another source for Bogie's off-camera avoidance of Bergman: his fear of his wife's jealousy. From the moment shooting began, "Sluggy" (Mayo Methot) Bogart was convinced her husband was having an affair with his leading lady. She called him repeatedly throughout the day to make sure the co-stars were not spending any extra time together and berated him about the affair through many a

Humphrey Bogart and Ingrid Bergman rehearse on the set. Off-camera contact between the two was rare. Not only did Bogie avoid Bergman throughout filming, for fear of angering his wife, but their paths rarely crossed socially. Between films, Bogart stayed in Hollywood, while Bergman joined her husband and daughter in Rochester, New York.

sleepless night. Rather than give her any further excuse to make his life miserable, Bogart simply chose to spend as little time as possible with Bergman.

He may have had another motivation as well. In an interview with Bergman's biographer Lawrence Leamer, one of the publicists on *Casablanca*, Bob William, noted that Bogie seemed to sulk every time William brought a male reporter on set to meet with Bergman. Women reporters elicited no response, but the sight of a male journalist with his co-star seemed to depress Bogie. In William's opinion, Bogart was, at the very least, infatuated with Bergman, but felt that their marital entanglements made any relationship beyond the professional impossible.

After three days of work on the Paris flashback, the company moved to the biggest and most expensive set built for *Casablanca*, Rick's Café Americain. The café consisted of several playing areas: a grand entrance, an outdoor terrace, the gambling room, the bar, the dining area where Sam and the orchestra

Bogart, Bergman, and Michael Curtiz during filming of Ilsa's late-night return to Rick's Café. Although at least one member of the Warner Bros. staff suspected Bogie of having a crush on his leading lady, there is no rumor of the director having designs on her. He was too busy seducing starlets.

played, and Rick's office. Rather than shoot each of these areas in isolation, however, Curtiz and Wallis decided to incorporate them all within one massive set, so the camera could follow the characters as they moved from one part of the café to the other. The cost of building Rick's Place was $9,200, more than half the film's $18,000 set budget.

Peter Lorre, Dan Seymour, and Madeleine LeBeau joined the company on the first day of filming in Rick's Café, May 28, 1942. Joy Page, Marcel Dalio, and Helmut Dantine started the following day. Claude Rains would not be finished with *Now, Voyager* until June 4, while Conrad Veidt would not be done playing MGM's *Nazi Agent* until June 8.

The biggest waits of all, however, were for Sydney Greenstreet and Paul Henreid. For Greenstreet, there was little problem. Señor Ferrari only had one scene at Rick's, and that could be shot any time the set was still up. Henreid, however, was a key player with several important scenes at the café. When *Now, Voyager* fell behind schedule, Henreid's arrival was delayed from early June until June 25. In the reports filed by Al Alleborn, he noted that Hen-

reid's absence had pushed the production behind schedule by as much as three days at one point. On June 9, there was even talk of recasting.

To compensate for Henreid's absence, Curtiz shot everything he could to get around the actor—not just the scenes in which he did not appear, but also other characters' reactions to Victor. At one point, Wallis sent Curtiz a memo complaining that there was no sense of rhythm to the rushes because the director could only shoot little bits and pieces.

Henreid's absence was not the only production problem. Wallis continued to object to Arthur Edeson's photography. The *Casablanca* correspondence files contain numerous memos in which Wallis complains that the lighting in Rick's Café is too bright. Repeatedly he urged Edeson to use more shadows to get a moodier look to the picture. In later memos, he addressed his concerns directly to Michael Curtiz. By this time (June 12), there was so much film shot with too much light that Wallis even authorized Curtiz to do retakes or print scenes darker to prevent any matching problems. Finally, Wallis tired of making the same complaint over and over again. In a memo dated June 15, he told Curtiz that it was up to him to

In one draft of CASABLANCA, Rick and Renault played chess while Victor and Ilsa's plane took off. Off-camera, the game was a popular pastime for (left to right) Claude Rains, Humphrey Bogart, and Paul Henreid.

make sure that the sets were properly lit.

Another problem was Dooley Wilson's inability to play the piano. Pianist Elliot Carpenter had been hired to record the piano tracks, which Wilson would mime. But Wilson had to be able to hear the piano, and Curtiz had decided to have dialogue overlap the music, even in shots where Wilson was clearly seen at the piano. The man in charge of playing back Carpenter's piano tracks followed standard procedure. When there was no dialogue, he played the prerecorded music at full volume, then took it out as soon as someone had to speak. But without the playback, Wilson was totally lost. Curtiz finally came up with a solution to the problem. He had Carpenter installed at a piano just out of camera range, so he could play as the camera rolled. Wilson could hear the music and sneak occasional peeks at Carpenter's playing to match his hand movements.

After hearing the recordings of the film's songs, Wallis began wondering if he should not have a singer with a more traditional crooner's voice as opposed to Wilson's raspier, jazz-oriented style. After all, "As Time Goes By" played a prominent part in the film's action, and the studio had great hopes that "Knock on

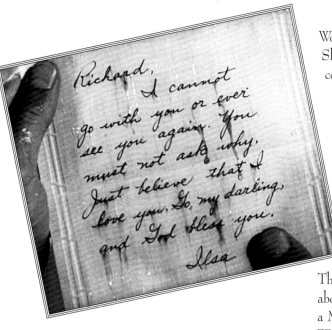

Wood," an original song written for the film, would become a hit. Should they hedge their bets by having the songs performed in a more conventional manner?

On July 3, Wallis sent a memo to Leo Forbstein, head of the studio's Music Department, requesting that he find a singer to dub Wilson's vocals. Fortunately, Wallis abandoned that idea.

Wallis may have had doubts about Dooley Wilson's singing, but there was no doubt in his mind about Leonid Kinsky's acting—he loathed it. After seeing the first rushes featuring the actor as Sascha, the bartender, Wallis wrote Curtiz on June 4, stating that he thought Kinsky was overplaying outrageously. With little time for retakes or recasting, he suggested putting more focus on Carl, the headwaiter, even though the role had yet to be cast. The writers had created a comic bit in which Sascha, eager to learn about how to make American drinks, follows a recipe for the creation of a Mickey Finn, then innocently gives it to one of the German officers. Wallis suggested either finding a way to give the bit to Carl or, as happened, cutting it altogether.

Wallis's day-to-day involvement with *Casablanca* also extended to decisions that, though they might seem insignificant today, helped refine the finished film. Orry-Kelly had planned to put Paul Henreid and Ingrid Bergman in evening clothes for their first entrance at Rick's Café, following the description of their entrance in *Everybody Comes to Rick's*. But on June 3, Wallis decided this would be out of character for a pair of refugees who had made a hurried escape from the Nazis in Paris and been on the road for some time. Instead, Henreid would wear "a plain sport outfit, or a palm beach suit" and Bergman would have "just a plain little street suit." Two days later, after viewing tests of Bergman in various hairstyles, Wallis notified Perc Westmore that the actress would wear her hair down, maintaining the natural look that had been established for her in *Intermezzo*.

On June 1 a revised script appeared, but it was not the approved final version. Still, the pages on file at the University of Southern California are closer to the finished film than anything that had come before. In this draft, Martinez's name has been changed to Ferrari to make it clear that the character is from Italy, one of the Axis countries, rather than neutral Spain. Ilsa's request that Sam play "As Time Goes By" has been restored, and three lines appear for the first time in their final forms (some already had been filmed): "If it's December 1941 in Casablanca, what time is it in New York?"; "Of all the gin joints in all the cities in all the world, she walks into mine"; and "Here's looking at you, kid." In addition, this is the first draft in which there is no implication of Rick's and Ilsa's sleeping together after the late-night confrontation in his apartment. Instead, they are interrupted by Carl's arrival with

While Wallis concerned himself with day-to-day details on the film, like the performance of Leonid Kinsky (top), whose work as Sascha he considered overdone, Jack Warner dealt more with the bottom line. Before filming began, he told Michael Curtiz to get CASABLANCA made in seven weeks. Later, he would write complaining of excessive takes, as in the memo above.

Victor, who has been wounded in the police raid on the resistance meeting.

The love triangle is not resolved in this draft. Though the action now takes place at Casablanca's airport, the script pages from the June 1 draft have been removed and replaced with pages dated July 15 and 16 that contain the scene as we know it today. The script then reverts to the June 1 pages, which are similar to the final film, up to a point. After letting Rick off the hook for shooting Strasser, Renault offers him a letter of transit out of Casablanca. Rick responds, "My letter of transit? I could use a trip…But it doesn't make any difference about our bet, Louis. You still owe me the ten thousand francs." At this point, the script ends, two lines short of what would be the screen ending.

The lack of a final script was causing problems on the production by this time. Starting June 5, Alleborn's reports on production delays begin making almost daily references to the need for a script so he could plan the rest of the shoot. A "final draft" was distributed June 24, but Jack Warner was not happy with it and called it back as soon as it had been released.

There were two major problems: Nobody was happy with the way Rick sent Ilsa off with Victor. No matter how many different ways they tried it, it seemed wrong, either too heartless or too contrived. And there was no way to end the scene, either. If Ilsa gave in and went away, she seemed wishy-washy. If Rick did anything to force her to leave, he seemed too hard.

As Wallis watched the early rushes, he became aware that something extraordinary was happening with Humphrey Bogart's performance. The producer had hoped the film would prove Bogie's potential as a romantic lead, and he was right. But this surprisingly strong performance raised a serious question. Would audiences accept this man's losing the woman he loved to someone else? Discussions began about other endings for the film: Rick takes Ilsa off to Lisbon; Ilsa stays with Rick in Casablanca; Rick is killed helping the Laszlos escape; Victor is shot, leaving the two lovers together.

Word of these discussions must have gotten to the actors, because they were beginning to express some anxiety over how the film would end. Bergman, in particular, argued that she needed to know what was going on so she could gauge how to play Ilsa's scenes with Rick and Victor. Which character should she lean toward to prepare for the ending? When she asked Curtiz for guidance, she never felt she got what she needed. On good days, he would respond with such helpful advice as, "Just play it…in between." Less helpful still was, "Just play it day to day, and we'll see what happens." But when pressed too often, Curtiz would lose all patience and rave, "Actors! Actors! They want to know everything!"

At least there were some moments that lightened the mood. On July 1, Hal Wallis halted shooting temporarily to throw a surprise party to celebrate the fifteenth anniversary of Curtiz's arrival at Warner Bros. The set filled with actors and technicians who had worked with the director, many of whom felt they owed him their careers. It was a wonderful, warm gesture, but it did little to solve the script problems.

Neither did Peter Lorre's antics. Though Lorre was only on set four days, he managed to create havoc while he was there. One of his silliest pranks was pulled on cinematographer Arthur Edeson. Edeson was a rarity among Hollywood cameramen in that he preferred to make his own chalk marks to show the actors where to stand. But as soon as the cameras had been set up, and Edeson's back was turned, Lorre would erase the chalk marks and make new ones. The cinematographer could not figure out why his setups never seemed to work.

Edeson was just a warm-up for the pranks Lorre had prepared for his director. Knowing Curtiz's reputation for getting fast-paced performances out of his actors, Lorre and Bogart decided to pull his leg. When Curtiz asked them to play their one scene at a rapid pace Bogie started to argue with the direction. But Lorre stood up for Curtiz, pointing out that if they played the scene fast enough they would not have to shoot on Friday, which would be in violation of their contracts. Curtiz stared at the two as they explained that they were not "weekend actors," but rather that their contracts expressly forbade their acting on Fridays, Saturdays, and Sundays. Seeing his entire production schedule go up in smoke, the director stalked off, yelling about "Weekend actors! God damn lousy bums!" When Friday rolled around, however, and the two actors reported to work, Curtiz was either too embarrassed or angry to admit that he had finally caught on to the joke. Perhaps he never did.

Bogart and Lorre also set out to create a feud between Curtiz and an old friend of his, Hungarian actor Paul Lukas. They told the director how much they admired his friend and pumped him for stories about Lukas. Then they went to a neighboring soundstage where Lukas was shooting *Watch on the Rhine* and asked Lukas what had happened to his friendship with Curtiz. They repeated the director's stories, but with enough changes to make them distinctly unflattering. Lukas responded by ranting about his supposed friend, rantings the two actors were only too happy to carry back to Curtiz. This went on for a few days until the relationship between Lukas and Curtiz was almost in shambles. Finally, Lorre and Bogart explained their trick and helped patch things up between the two friends.

But this was hardly the limit of how far Lorre would go. Curtiz was notorious for his wandering eye. Using his position at Warner Bros. as a persuasive tool, he had no trouble finding ambitious women who would bed him for a shot at the big time. A married man, Curtiz usually had to schedule these liaisons during breaks in shooting. He even had his own dressing trailer on the set, where he could engage in his lunchtime dalliances.

One day, Lorre slipped a microphone into Curtiz's little hideaway. During lunch, some of the cast and crew stuck around to listen to the director's lovemaking, a curious collection of moans and groans punc-

Humphrey Bogart was a willing accomplice in many of Peter Lorre's practical jokes. When Bogie learned his drinking buddy had been cast, the two began planning the many ways they would bedevil Mike Curtiz during Lorre's four days of shooting.

tuated with impassioned, thickly accented cries of, "Oh, God, no!" and "Oh, God, yes!"

In all, the company remained in Rick's Café on Soundstage 8 for six weeks, with only two-and-a-half days of work on other sets. By June 3, the train station from *Now, Voyager* was available and had been transformed into the Paris Gare, so Bogart and Wilson filmed the flashback scene in which Rick learns that Ilsa will not be leaving with him. In addition, Bogart and Bergman did some retakes of the scene in Ilsa's Paris apartment. On July 3, Bogart and Bergman shot some additional closeups in the Montmartre Café, and did some other scenes at

Rick's Café as well. And on July 10, Conrad Veidt and Claude Rains finally got to work on the film's one location scene, Major Strasser's arrival at the Casablanca airport.

One of the most popular shooting locations in the Hollywood area was the Los Angeles Metropolitan Airport in Van Nuys. It was here that the company adjourned on July 10 after the construction of a set piece to serve as the entrance to the Casablanca airport and following a great deal of schedule juggling by production manager Alleborn, who had to both arrange for a day when they could shoot at the busy airport and find a plane that looked right for the landing shot. They found what they wanted in a hangar in Arizona and had its exterior refurbished to look appropriately Teutonic.

Fortunately, Curtiz got the airport scene finished in the single day allotted for it, filming around other takeoffs and landings. It would be the director's only day at the airport. The night shots of Ilsa and Victor's plane taking off would be done by a second-unit crew about two weeks later.

On July 11, Curtiz shot some pick-up scenes at Rick's Café, then moved to the sets for Renault's and Strasser's offices. On Wallis's orders, the set for Rick's was left up for a few days, until he and Curtiz were sure they would need no more retakes there, then dismantled. As the cast moved on to film Victor and Ilsa's departure from Casablanca, their meeting with Señor Ferrari at the Blue Parrot and Ilsa's late-night visit to Rick's apartment, the set pieces and properties from Rick's Café were returned to the Warner Bros. Props and Scenery departments and the various places from which they had been borrowed.

By the end of shooting on Soundstage 8, several cast members had finished their work on the film. Peter Lorre shot his last scene on June 2, with Marcel Dalio finishing up one week after that. Rick's rejected girlfriend, Yvonne, was set free June 27, followed by Sascha, the love-sick bartender, one day later. Corinna Mura strummed her guitar in Casa-

PubA9

The Jokester Is Wild

Peter Lorre's incessant practical joking made him a terror in the business, if a highly regarded one. In fact, it was a joke—making fun of a pamphlet he had been asked to read at a Nazi rally—that led to his flight from Germany. But he met his match in the master of suspense Alfred Hitchcock.

After finishing their second film together, *Secret Agent*, Hitchcock set sail for America, only to be confronted with a stateroom filled with canaries, a going-away present Lorre had arranged. Not to be outdone, the director proceeded to send Lorre almost hourly telegrams about how each and every bird was doing, guaranteeing that the actor would not sleep a wink until Hitchcock arrived in New York.

Don't Rains On My Parade

Peter Lorre and Humphrey Bogart were not the only cast members to pull an occasional joke at Mike Curtiz's expense. Late in the picture, Claude Rains, as Captain Renault, arrives at Rick's Café, where he thinks he will be arresting Victor Laszlo. Curtiz wanted the scene played at a rapid pace, both to capture Renault's excitement at finally getting the goods on Laszlo and to keep the tension flowing as the film moved toward its climax. He instructed Rains to pound on the door, then rush past Rick when he opened it for him.

The scene was the first to be shot that day, however, and the early morning hours were not the best time for Rains to be playing anything quite that energetic. As take followed take, Curtiz began losing patience with the British actor. Finally, to break the tension, Rains enlisted Bogart's cooperation in giving the director too much of what he wanted. The next time the cameras rolled, Bogart opened the door and Rains came in fast all right—on a bicycle. After everybody had a good laugh, they finally got the scene to Curtiz's satisfaction.

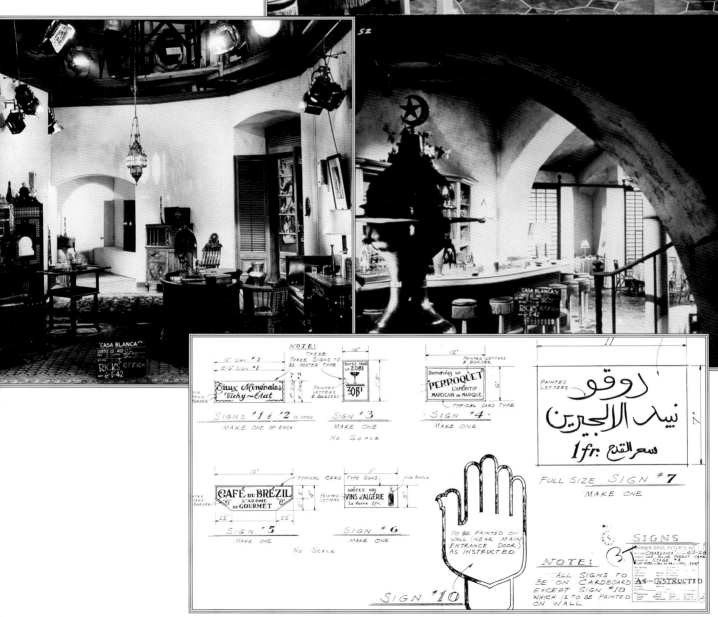

Rick's Café Americain was constructed on Soundstage 8 and represented the largest set used in the film, including the restaurant and bar (above), Rick's office (middle row left and right), and the balcony outside his office (middle row center). The designers also came up with a suitably classy entrance (above right), which figures prominently in the publicity shot at right with Henreid, Bergman, and Bogart. The company spent six weeks filming here, more than on any other set. They spent only a few days at the Blue Parrot, actually a set from THE DESERT SONG that was redecorated with new signs (left).

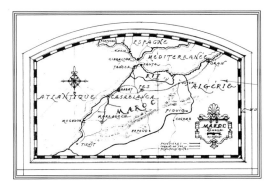

From Rick's Café, the company moved to scenes set in Renault's and Strasser's offices (top and left). The former was dominated by a wall-sized map of Morocco (design above), or "Maroc" as the French called it. OPPOSITE: Rick and Victor during the singing of "La Marseillaise."

blanca for the last time July 1, and Rick's Arab bodyguard, played by Dan Seymour, was discharged July 2, the same day Dooley Wilson finished his role. The last member of the café staff to finish shooting was S. Z. Sakall. Wallis had added a scene between Sakall and Henreid at the back door to Rick's, just after the resistance meeting. The scene, which used pieces of the barroom set to create a sparse background for the two, required Sakall to remain with the production until July 9.

The next scenes shot—set in Strasser's and Renault's offices and the Laszlos' Casablanca hotel room—went by with few problems, giving the company a much-needed respite. On July 17, four-and-a-half days behind schedule and still without an ending, the shooting moved to Soundstage 1 for the late-night scene at the Casablanca Airport, the setting for the film's finale.

The set had been created with the same painstaking care that had gone into the filming of every other scene in *Casablanca*. Warners' new fog machines—introduced on Curtiz's previous film, *The Sea Wolf*—were working overtime to create atmosphere from more than half-a-million cubic feet of vaporized oil, in sublime ignorance of the fact that the desert-bound North African city hardly ever saw a day of fog in its history. Props had secured a bottle of Vichy water, strategically placed for Captain Renault to pick up at a tense moment. The Costume Department had Bogart's trench coat and snap-brim hat ready to become a permanent part of his mystique. The carpenters had built the interior of the hangar, complete with the telephone at which Strasser would make his last stand. And they had also constructed a believable twin-engine Air France plane, scaled down in size to create the illusion that the studio air strip was larger than it actually was. Casting had even recruited some midgets to sit in the dummy plane's windows to add to the illusion.

Foremost in everyone's mind, however, was the resolution of the romantic triangle. Various endings were discussed, but each had its

Giving Bogie the Nod

One of the many little bits Michael Curtiz filmed while waiting for Paul Henreid to be available was a simple shot of Bogart on the steps leading from his office down to the main room at Rick's Café. When the actor arrived for that day's shooting, Curtiz told him that all he had to do was stand there and nod in a certain direction. Bogie wanted to know what he was nodding for, but Curtiz just snapped, "Don't ask so many questions. Get up there and nod, and then go home." It was not until he saw the film that the actor knew what he was doing. His nod was the signal to the orchestra to start *"La Marseillaise"* in one of *Casablanca*'s most fondly remembered scenes.

DÉFENSE ABSOLUE
DE FUMER

"CASABLANCA"
CURTIZ CO. 410
STAGE # LOCATION SC-263
SET STILL
EXT- AIRPORT
DATE 7-17-42

LEFT: The set for the airport and hangar, constructed on Soundstage I. Note the bottles of Vichy water below the desk, right, and the telephone stand, center, at which Major Strasser would be shot. The car (above right) that carried Rick and the Laszlos to the airport has a current asking price of $35,000.

problems. If Ilsa chose to stay with Rick, there would be hell to pay with the MPPDA. Although it might happen in real life, in Hollywood in the 1940s a good wife simply did not leave her husband for another man, no matter how charismatic the interloper might be. Having Rick killed as the Laszlos escaped might be too grim for audiences. And after all the work Wallis, Curtiz, and the writers had done to give Bogart a new, more romantic image, having him die before the final fadeout would be like returning to the earlier films in which he had played more villainous roles. Killing Victor, on the other hand, would leave his anti-Nazi work unfinished and severely undermine the story's political ramifications.

Fortunately, somebody came up with the solution: Rick would send Ilsa off, not because he was weak and had nothing to offer her, but because her work with Victor was too important to sacrifice at this point. It was the one argument she could not dispute and the only one that did not damage the strength of Rick's, or Bogie's, character. To make sure Ilsa could not protest, the writers contrived to have Victor interrupt the farewell just as Rick had finished making his case.

It is hard to say who came up with the ending. The Epsteins were the only writers assigned to the film at the time this scene was shot, so they are the most likely candidates for the honor. However, Casey Robinson's earlier memo on rewriting the romantic scenes suggests that, at the very least, he might have provided the idea for the ending. According to Robinson the resolution of the love triangle should force Ilsa "to carry on with the work that in these days is far more important than the love of two little people."

According to one of the many legends about the making of *Casablanca*, there also was another ending written, one in which Ilsa stays with Rick. Supposedly, Curtiz was going to shoot this one as well so that Wallis could decide which he preferred.

There are two factors arguing against this legend. For one thing, no such pages exist in the University of Southern California files on the film. Second, such an ending would have changed more than just the scene between Bogart and Bergman; it would have altered everything to follow. At an economy-minded studio like Warners, it would not have been feasible to add four to five days of shooting to a schedule that already was behind.

The script pages for *Casablanca*'s new ending (or endings) had been delivered the night before the scene was to be shot, and unit manager Al Alleborn reported that filming was moving slowly because the actors simply had not had enough time to learn the lines. Also delaying the filming was an argument between Bogart and Curtiz that finally had to be resolved by Hal Wallis. Alleborn's production report does not state specifically what the subject was, but accounts from those involved with

the film indicated that they disagreed about whether or not Rick should kiss Ilsa. Curtiz wanted to go the more conventional route and give his two leading players one final kiss before parting. Bogart argued that such a move would contradict everything he had just said to send Ilsa away. Wallis sided with Bogart.

The Public Relations Department put a sunny face on the whole squabble by issuing a lighthearted press release stating: "[Humphrey Bogart's] chance came today, and he turned it down.

He said, no, he wouldn't kiss Ingrid Bergman....

'Look, don't get the idea I am turning soft. But if we stick to the story, the guy I am playing would have to give a thought or two to the husband. He'd be thinking that any second the guy might come busting through the door and shoot first and ask questions later.

'I am a guy like this, when I play kissing games I want to give the matter my undivided attention.'"

Another problem occurred when Curtiz began berating one of the bit players. The director had a habit of singling out one performer on each production, usually someone in a smaller part, as the scapegoat for his frustrations. On *Casablanca*, it was an English actor whom everybody agreed was not terribly good. Early in the shooting, however, Claude Rains had had enough of Curtiz's bullying and had gotten together with Bogart and Henreid to discuss the situation. They went to Curtiz and told him how much it bothered them to see anybody, however inept, treated so rudely. Curtiz, of course, was all apologies. He had not realized how much it bothered them, and he promised to keep his temper. Just to make sure, they threatened to walk off the film if anything like that happened again.

While shooting the airport scene, however, Curtiz forgot his promise. There were difficulties getting the first shot. The car carrying Rick, Victor, Ilsa, and Renault had to drive to

284. CLOSE SHOT RICK

as he returns Renault's gaze. His eyes are expressionless.

285. FULL SHOT

The gendarmes run to Renault. Renault turns to them.

RENAULT:
Major Strasser has been shot.
(pauses as he looks at Rick, then to the gendarmes:)
Round up the usual suspects...

GENDARME:
(saluting)
Yes, Captain.

He leads the other gendarmes off. The two men look at one another.

RICK: ~~Thanks, Louis.~~

RENAULT: Perhaps you're right
(lights a cigarette)
Ricky, until this affair dies down, it might be just as well for you to disappear from Casablanca. I understand there's a Free French garrison over at Bravvaville. If you're interested, I might be induced to arrange your passage.

RICK:
(smiles)
My Letter of Transit?
(his eyes following the plane, which is now receding into the distance)
I could use a trip... But it doesn't make any difference about our bet, Louis. You still owe me the ten thousand francs.

RENAULT

— and that ten thousand should just about pay our expenses.

FADE OUT.

THE END

a mark and stop, and the cast had to get out in the right order, all the while spitting out the lines at a rapid pace. But every time they tried it, something went wrong. The car missed its mark. The actors did not get out right. The lines were too slow. Finally, everything went right until Curtiz's pet actor garbled his line.

The director turned on him with a rant of truly heroic proportions—and his three male stars walked off the set. According to Henreid, they actually enjoyed hiding out, making Curtiz look for them and, finally, getting him to apologize. After several hours away from the set, they eventually allowed their director to talk them back into shooting the scene.

With Ilsa and Victor safely on their way to Lisbon, attention turned to the next problem with the script, what to do with Rick, Renault, and Strasser. Rick was supposed to shoot Strasser as the German officer ran to the phone to try to stop the plane. But the MPPDA had insisted that Strasser's shooting be clearly depicted as self-defense, so the writers inserted a stage direction in which Strasser pulls a gun on Rick as he gets to the phone. The scene was shot, and Veidt and Rains were released from the film. But when Wallis saw the rushes he did not think the self-defense angle was clear enough. So, the two actors were called back to do the scene again.

They finally finished their roles on July 22, the last day of filming on the airport set.

The handling of Strasser's death led logically to the next issue that needed to be resolved, the relationship between Rick and Renault. After covering up Strasser's killing, the Vichy police officer was in as much danger in Casablanca as Rick. Since Koch had earlier introduced the idea of placing Renault between his friendship with Rick and his forced allegiance to France's German conquerors, the perfect resolution would be for Renault to join the resistance with Rick at the film's end.

In fact, this would prove to be a popular ending politically, as it showed the Free French spirit rising up to fight the Third Reich. It

would also, however, lead to an unintentional error in the film. Renault suggests that he and Rick join the Free French garrison in Brazzaville; then they start walking across the airfield, in the opposite direction from which their car had come. The move makes it seem that Brazzaville is where they are headed as the end titles come up. The only problem is that Brazzaville is located in the Congo, approximately a thousand miles from Casablanca.

When shooting on the airport set finished July 22, the company was eight days behind schedule. Only two elements about the scene were left incomplete. The second-unit company had been scheduled to film the take-off of Victor and Ilsa's plane on July 20 at the Metropolitan Airport, but the shoot had been postponed when somebody noticed that the plane they had engaged for the scene did not have the same number of windows as the model plane on the set. A different plane was secured (a twin-engine Lockheed Electra 12A), and the scene was finished on July 23. The same day, not taking any chances, Wallis sent a memo to the film's editor, Owen Marks, advising him to make sure Rick and Renault were looking off after the Laszlos' plane in the same direction in which it had departed.

The other unresolved matter was the film's final line. This would not delay production. The line would play with an overhead shot of the two characters, so it could be dubbed in by Bogart well after shooting was completed.

As the scene draws to an end, Rick reminds Renault that, "You still owe me ten thousand francs," the payment due on their bet over whether or not Victor Laszlo would get out of Casablanca. Renault then states, "And that ten thousand francs should pay our expenses," an indication that he will be accompanying Rick to Brazzaville. Wallis then had four possibilities to choose from for the final line: 1) "Louis, I begin to see a reason for your sudden attack of patriotism. While you defend your country, you also protect your investment."; 2) "If you ever die a hero's death, Heaven protect

WARNER BROS. PICTURES, INC.
BURBANK, CALIFORNIA

INTER-OFFICE COMMUNICATION

DATE July 23, 1942

SUBJECT "CASABLANCA"

TO MR. OWEN MARKS

FROM MR. WALLIS

Will you please check the miniature shots of the plane taking off from the Casablanca Airport in the fog and see if the direction is right to match it with the direction in which Rick and Rains look off as they are walking out of the Airport near the end of the picture.

Let me know, as the Miniature Department wants to strike the set and I don't want to do this until I am sure that what we have will cut out properly.

HAL WALLIS

ABOVE: Struck by last-minute misgivings, Hal Wallis asks CASABLANCA's editor, Owen Marks, to be sure Victor and Ilsa's plane takes off in the same direction Rick and Renault are looking. LEFT: Renault, Rick, and the Laszlos arrive at the Casablanca airport. The bit player (left) was the likely recipient of one of Curtiz's most impressive temper tantrums, an outburst that led Rains, Bogart, and Henreid to walk off the set for several hours.

the angels!"; 3) "Louis, I might have known you'd mix your patriotism with a little larceny."; or 4) "Louis, I think this is the beginning of a beautiful friendship."

Wallis had plenty of time to make up his mind. The line was not scheduled for dubbing until late August, after Bogart had finished the film and taken a brief vacation. By August 7, he had narrowed the decision down to the last two choices. By August 21, he settled on the last one. Ironically, the author of that line was Hal Wallis himself.

Contrary to legend, the filming of the airport scene in *Casablanca* did not mark the end of shooting for the film or its stars. There would be eleven more days of work on the picture, almost two weeks. And contrary to Bergman's later stories of never knowing which of the two men she would be leaving with until all the other scenes had been shot, she actually filmed some of her most important scenes with Bogart and Henreid after she knew which would win her.

By July 23, the *Desert Song* company had finally finished with the set that would become the Blue Parrot, the rival club run by Sydney Greenstreet as Señor Ferrari. There had been several delays in getting to the set as shooting of *The Desert Song* dragged on. These delays, in turn, had caused problems for *Casablanca*.

Greenstreet's contract for the film called for a minimum of two weeks' work. But with no set on which to play his scenes, his commitment to the film had dragged on for an additional week and a half, at the healthy sum of $3,750 per week.

Alleborn's explanation of why they needed the actor for extra time explains a lot about the problems of scheduling a film shoot. Greenstreet had finished his scene at Rick's Café in one day, but they could not move to other sets right away as the cost of keeping up the massive set for Rick's was much higher than Greenstreet's salary. And they could not move

straight to the Blue Parrot set when they were done at Rick's because, one, it wasn't available and two, Alleborn needed to schedule Rains's and Veidt's last scenes as soon as possible—each of those actors was costing the film more than Greenstreet. When the Blue Parrot set was finally available, Greenstreet finished his part in three days.

On July 27, Bergman and Bogart began shooting one of their most important scenes together, her visit to his apartment to get the exit visas. Amazingly, this difficult scene was completed in only a day and a half, followed by half a day shooting Ilsa's scene with Victor in their Casablanca hotel room. Still, the company was now ten days behind.

Filming moved to the Black Market on July 30, with the stars having two days off while Curtiz directed Joy Page, Helmut Dantine, and numerous extras in scenes to be added to the opening montage. Originally, Wallis and Curtiz had budgeted for 152 extras in this sequence, but faced with the production's many costly delays, they cut the number to 90.

One more brief delay was caused by Curtiz's mangled English. On the day he arrived to shoot the first Black Market scene, he informed the properties man, who already had assembled an impressive group of animals for the shot, that he needed a "poodle, a black poodle." The request seemed unusual, but the prop man was not about to argue with the temperamental director, so he set about finding the dog while everyone waited.

As luck would have it, there was just such an animal available, and the man got it to the set within half an hour. "It's very nice," said Curtiz, "but I want a poodle." When the poor technician tried to explain that that's what the dog was, Curtiz exploded: "I wanted a poodle in the street! A poodle of water! Not a goddamn dog!"

Ingrid Bergman returned to film her

Include *Me* Out, Too

command of the English language coupled with a thick Hungarian accent. During one film with Errol Flynn, the director asked his star to play a line with "a tinkle in your eye." On *Casablanca*, he tried to motivate Ingrid Bergman for a romantic scene by telling her to imagine "the beating of the native tom-thumbs." On another Flynn picture, he was trying to get the seamen on one ship to swing over to the decks of the other and attack convincingly. "Lunge! Lunge!" he shouted in his thick Hungarian accent, only to stand dumbfounded as the entire cast and crew left the soundstage. They thought he was sending them to lunch.

Many apocryphal stories about Curtiz's funniest lines probably resulted from his temper's getting the better of him. When an assistant bungled an errand, Curtiz stormed, "The next time I send a dumb son of a bitch, I go myself!" Confronted with too much noise on the set, he shouted, "Anybody who has any talking to do, please shut up!"

One of the trademarks of Curtiz's directing style was his ability to find a single object that would sum up the action of a scene or even the entire movie, as when Claude Rains discards a bottle of Vichy water at the end of *Casablanca*. This practice gave Curtiz one of his most famous slips of the tongue, when he decided he wanted a shot of a riderless horse towards the end of *The Charge of the Light Brigade*. "Bring me an empty horse," he ordered, thus giving the film's co-star, David Niven, the title for the second volume of his memoirs.

Curtiz was not always amused with his notoriety in this area. He accused the press of trying to make him sound like "a jingle bells," and when one reporter too many asked him to say something funny he responded in perfect Curtiz style, "I say something funny all right. I say a three-letter word beginning with 'f.'"

W hen it came to mangling the English language, director Michael Curtiz bowed to no one, with the possible exception of independent producer Samuel Goldwyn. And like Goldwyn's PR department, the Warners publicists did their best to make sure that Curtiz's most colorful—and more repeatable—pronouncements made it into the press.

Curtiz's problem was twofold, a shaky

Black Market confrontation with Bogart on August 1, a day that would become one of the most important in her life. She finished the scene and moved on to a publicity shoot with Paul Henreid, but her spirits were noticeably down. Thinking she was having romantic troubles, he asked what the problem was. It was not an affair of the heart, she explained. She was depressed because the film was almost completed, and she had no other roles lined up. Particularly upsetting was the knowledge that *For Whom the Bell Tolls* had already started filming with Vera Zorina in the part Bergman craved.

Zorina's performance in the first rushes had been a disaster. She looked terrible in short hair and, to make matters worse, she tiptoed around the mountainous location like a ballerina, which, in point of fact, she was, afraid of injuring her most important assets. The situation with Zorina was so bad that Bergman had been called in to make a secret screen test (though everybody in town knew about it) on July 31. But she was convinced that Paramount would not want to re-shoot Zorina's scenes. As far as she was concerned, she had once again lost what would have been the most important role in her career.

During the publicity shoot with Henreid, Bergman was called to the phone to speak to David O. Selznick. His message was simple: "Ingrid, you are Maria!" She returned to the shoot a different person, ready to celebrate her greatest victory.

Wallis knew about Bergman's casting in *For Whom the Bell Tolls* before the contracts were signed. He had been asked to release her as soon as possible, so he and Curtiz arranged to screen as much of the film as had been assembled to make sure they would not need their leading lady for any retakes.

Casablanca finished shooting on August 3 with some shots of Bergman and Henreid in the Blue Parrot and the Black Market and a few more crowd scenes. The last official shot printed was one of the first that appears in the film, the scene in which a crowd of refugees watches the

Lisbon plane pass by overhead. It was the 744th shot taken for the film. In all, the shoot lasted almost ten weeks, and came in eleven days behind schedule. Total cost was approximately $950,000.

Wallis and Curtiz viewed the film on August 4, and though Wallis wanted to add a brief scene, it did not involve Bergman. On August 5, she was released to begin work on *For Whom the Bell Tolls*. The first thing she did was to get her hair cut, an act that would have unexpected repercussions on the future of *Casablanca*.

Though the leading lady had been released, Wallis's work on *Casablanca* was far from over. By the end of August, Bogart had recorded the new last line. On August 22, Curtiz put in his last day of filming, shooting the scene Wallis had added at the police station: a medium closeup of a police officer reading a teletype report about the murder of two German couriers and the theft of the exit visas they were carrying. It would be one of the first scenes in the finished film.

Now it was time for Owen Marks and Max Steiner to start editing and scoring the film, respectively, but there was no hurry. Wallis was not planning to put *Casablanca* into release until spring of 1943.

As had been the case with the other Warners films he had worked on, Marks was charged with making *Casablanca* play as tightly as possible without any sacrifice of overall effect. In doing so, he had the benefit of Wallis's practiced eye. Many of the producer's editing notes are concerned with keeping up the pace. Marks was instructed to trim a few frames from closeups of the refugees, cut a few bars out of "Knock on Wood" so the Rick-Ferrari scene could start sooner, and get Carl from the gambling room entrance to Rick's table in less time than it actually took to make the cross.

ABOVE: Hal Wallis expected "Knock On Wood," an original song by M. K. Jerome and Jack Scholl, to be CASABLANCA's big musical hit. The success of "As Time Goes By" was a surprise to many at Warners. OPPOSITE: Major Strasser (Condrad Veidt) leads the singing of "Wacht am Rhein."

Wallis also had a keen eye for setting magical moments. As Ron Haver points out in his *American Film* article on *Casablanca*'s creation, the scene in which Ilsa asks Sam to play "As Time Goes By" is five lines shorter on film than it was on paper. The shooting script represented a considerable reduction from the scene in the original play, but was still a rather wordy introduction to one of the film's key moments:

ILSA: Play it, Sam. Play "As Time Goes By."

SAM: I can't remember it, Miss Ilsa. I'm a little rusty on it.

ILSA: I'll hum it for you.

SAM: I can't seem to get it.

ILSA: Somehow I didn't think that you would. I'll play it for you.

SAM: No, Miss Ilsa, I think I've got it now. (*SAM starts to play.*)

ILSA: Sing it, Sam.

SAM: I don't know the words.

ILSA: I'll sing them to you. "You must remember this…"

SAM: (*Picks up the song*) "You must remember this
A kiss is still a kiss
A sigh is just a sigh…"

On seeing that scene in the projection room, Wallis knew that it was slightly overwritten and asked Marks to cut around the lines and add a silent closeup of Bergman:

ILSA: Play it, Sam. Play "As Time Goes By."

SAM: I can't remember it, Miss Ilsa. I'm a little rusty on it.

ILSA: I'll hum it for you. (*SAM starts to play.*) Sing it, Sam.

SAM: (*Pause*) "You must remember this
A kiss is still a kiss
A sigh is just a sigh…"

With A Song In My Part

esides "As Time Goes By," other songs performed at Rick's Café included "If I Could Be With You," "It Had to Be You," "Shine," and "Sweet Georgia Brown," all performed by Dooley Wilson. Wilson also got to sing an original song, "Knock on Wood," which Wallis expected to be the big hit from the film.

Corinna Mura performed two Latin American numbers, *"Tabu"* and *"Tango des Roses,"* the latter obtained for a one-time payment of $180.00. But it was the German song drowned out by *"La Marseillaise"* that would cause Wallis the most trouble. In *Everybody Comes to Rick's*, the German officers sang the *"Horst Wessel,"* and originally

Wallis and the writers went along with that. But the Warners Legal Department informed Wallis that the song was still under copyright protection in Germany.

The song was then changed to *"Wacht am Rhein,"* which was conveniently in the public domain. During the first days of shooting, however, Wallis learned that the song was not in favor with the Nazi party. Studio Production Manager Tenny Wright solved the problem by pointing out that many high-ranking German officers actually disliked Hitler, thinking of themselves as Germans first and Nazis second. For them, singing a song out of favor with their Führer would be an acceptable act of defiance, particularly since they were stationed several hundred miles south of Berlin.

As Haver notes, Wallis's cutting created a moment that is still met "with absolute breathless silence as it unfolds, a moment that, in its own way, transfigures one as much as anything out of Wagner and Puccini."

Incredibly, that magical moment almost got deleted from the picture—and definitely would have been had Max Steiner had his way. Steiner had been assigned to the film on July 12, about three weeks before shooting finished. This was not at all unusual. In most cases, the scorer did not go to work until the film was completed and a rough cut had been assembled.

When Steiner started on the score he composed original themes with brief names like "Africa," "Bitterness," and "Nazi Spy." These would be combined with music from a variety of sources, including melodies that would evoke strong associations in the audience—like the German and French national anthems and the songs performed at Rick's Café. And that was the sticking point: Steiner did not like the most important song in the picture, "As Time Goes By."

For one thing, he felt that the song's six-note theme was too simple and was repeated too often to make it very useful as a motif for Rick and Ilsa's love. For another, he had just had a big hit with "It Can't Be Wrong," the original song he had written as a theme for Bette Davis and Paul Henreid in *Now, Voyager*. Naturally, the composer wanted another crack at a hit.

Steiner took his objections to Wallis and stated his case so persuasively that the producer gave in. But "As Time Goes By" was mentioned so frequently in the film that changing the song would require some retakes, particularly of the scene between Ilsa and Sam. And that was where the trouble lay.

OPPOSITE, BOTTOM RIGHT: Sam, Rick, and Ilsa "take the sting out of being occupied." BELOW AND OPPOSITE, TOP RIGHT: Sheet music for "As Time Goes By"

Ingrid Bergman had already cut her hair for her role in *For Whom the Bell Tolls*. Wallis got one look at her drastically shorter hairdo and realized that retakes would be impossible. They could have tried a wig, of course, but with no surety that it could be made to match Bergman's natural hair in the rest of the picture, the change simply was not worth the time and money.

Being an industry professional, Steiner accepted defeat gracefully and proved, contrary to his objections, that the melody from "As Time Goes By" could be easily adapted to a variety of settings throughout the score. In fact, it would become one of the most memorable movie themes of the forties. By the time the picture opened and became a hit, the composer even grudgingly admitted, in an interview with *PM* magazine, that though he still did not think much of the song, there must have been something good about it to capture the attention that it did.

It was standard practice in the Hollywood of the thirties and forties to "sneak" upcoming releases onto the bills at theaters in the Los Angeles area. Audience members were asked to fill out preview cards, and the various executives in attendance combined these with their own impressions to determine if any changes needed to be made in the picture before its premiere. At some studios, this previewing became a fine art. During the thirties, MGM was nicknamed "retake valley" because of the extensive changes production chief Irving G. Thalberg often ordered after previews. Money-conscious Warner Bros. did not go quite that far, but the studio would still make adjustments based on initial audience reactions.

Casablanca's first previews took place on September 22, 1942, in Huntington Park and

You Must Remember This

A s Time Goes By" is such an integral part of *Casablanca*, both the film and the legend, that many fans are surprised to discover that the song was not written specifically for the movie. In fact, it is one of the film's many carry-overs from Murray Burnett and Joan Allison's play *Everybody Comes to Rick's*.

The song was written by Herman Hupfield for a 1931 stage revue called *Everybody's Welcome*, where it was introduced by singer Frances White. It enjoyed a degree of popularity and had a few recordings, most notably one by Rudy Vallee. One of these got into the hands of Burnett while he was a student at Cornell University. It was love-at-first-listen for the future playwright, who played the recording so often that his fraternity brothers threatened him with physical violence.

By 1940, when Burnett and Allison were writing *Everybody Comes to Rick's*, Burnett wanted to give the song a second life as Rick and Lois's theme, the song they used to listen to in Paris at La Belle Aurore (another Burnett touch, the club had been his favorite hangout in Paris). When the play was sold to Hollywood, nobody thought of giving Rick and Ilsa another motif, particularly since "As Time Goes By" had been published by Warners' musical division and Wallis could get the rights—for a song.

CHORUS
You must remember this,
A kiss is still a kiss,
A sigh is just a sigh;
The fundamental things apply
As time goes by.

And when two lovers woo,
They still say, "I love you,"
On that you can rely;
No matter what the future
   brings
As time goes by.

Moonlight and love songs, never out of date,
Hearts full of passion, jealousy and hate;
Woman needs man, and man must have his mate,
That no one can deny.

It's still the same old story,
A fight for love and glory,
A case of do or die.
The world will always welcome lovers
As time goes by.

Mythmaking: Fact to Ficton

In *Everybody Comes to Rick's*:
"Play it, you dumb bastard."
In *Casablanca*, first draft:
"Play it, you dumb..."
In *Casablanca*, second draft:
"Play it!"
In *Casablanca*, the film:
"If she can stand it I can. Play it!"
Finally, in *Casablanca*, the myth:
"Play it again, Sam."

Pasadena, California. Although the preview cards are not on file at the University of Southern California, the prevailing opinion is that the film had only a mixed success. It is quite possible that at the time the audience did not know enough about *Casablanca*'s North African setting to appreciate everything that was going on. In fact, one executive suggested that Wallis revert to the original play's title because people would think "Casablanca" was a Mexican beer.

Wallis also got some encouraging notes. Charles Einfield, director of publicity and advertising for Warners, said the film would surely be "one of the hottest money pictures of the last two or three seasons." And Joseph I. Breen, who had kept Rick, Ilsa, and Renault on the straight and narrow, was so enthusiastic about the film that Wallis suggested Einfield speak to him to get ideas for how to market it.

As Wallis was fighting to keep *Casablanca* true to his vision, history stepped in to help. In November 1942, the Allies landed in North Africa and, in the Battle of Casablanca and other engagements, scored the first Allied success in the European theater. The effect on the nation was tremendous. Casablanca was in the news almost daily, sparking a tremendous interest in the exotic locale. Fashion designers even began inserting Moroccan and Tunisian motifs into their lines.

On November 6, Wallis sent Jack Warner a *San Francisco Chronicle* article about Casablanca's increasing prominence in the war news. This was an opportunity they could not afford to ignore.

Executives in Warners' New York sales office came up with the brilliant idea of adding an epilogue to the film. Rick and Renault would be shown in military uniform on an Allied ship, listening to Roosevelt's address to the Allies just before landing. Warner tried to talk the New York office out of ordering the

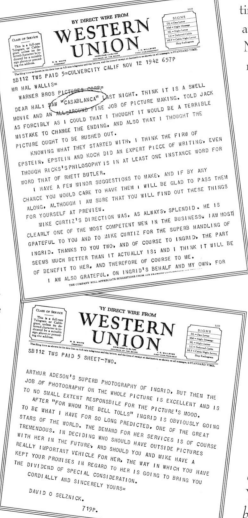

OPPOSITE: Victor tries to get Ilsa to reveal her feelings for Rick in another major scene Ingrid Bergman shot after she knew how the film would end.
BELOW: David O. Selznick's telegrams to Hall Wallis after seeing Casablanca.

change, stating that the picture should be released as soon as possible to capitalize on the title, but they would not budge. So Wallis ordered a set built, requisitioned a tape of Roosevelt's speech, and called Claude Rains back from his Pennsylvania farmhouse to shoot the scene.

But for a lucky break—named David O. Selznick—the ending of *Casablanca* might have been changed forever. Selznick had requested a screening of the film with a few of his executives, and it was set up for some time after November 13. Instead, he attended another preview held on November 11. Selznick was tremendously enthusiastic about the picture, as was the audience. In a telegram to Wallis, he thanked the producer for his "superb handling of Ingrid." He also stated that he "told Jack [Warner] as forcibly as I could that I thought it would be a terrible mistake to change the ending, and also that I thought the picture ought to be rushed out."

That was the ammunition Warner and Wallis needed. Warner advised the New York executives that on the basis of the preview no further changes would be made to the picture. Prints of the film were shipped overseas so the Allied soldiers in Casablanca would be the first to see the picture. In the U.S., the only booking available on such short notice was at New York's Hollywood Theatre. *Casablanca* was scheduled to premiere there on Thanksgiving Day, November 26, 1942—just eighteen days after the Allied landing—with a general release set for January 1943. That schedule would prove to be another key element in making *Casablanca* a classic.

Chapter Six

This Is The

BEGINNING

Of A Beautiful

FRIENDSHIP

The Fighting French march outside New York's Hollywood Theatre to celebrate CASABLANCA's premiere. Although the U.S. government had still not officially recognized the Free French, Hollywood's favorable treatment of the resistance in films like CASABLANCA would do a great deal to sway public opinion in their favor.

The premiere of *Casablanca* in November 1942 did indeed mark the beginning of a beautiful friendship between the film and its audiences, the film and its critics, and the film and Hollywood. From the New York opening, Warner Bros. took full advantage of *Casablanca*'s timely title and the topical elements of its story. The premiere was a gala event sponsored by France Forever and the Fighting French Relief Committee, which staged a parade for Foreign Legionnaires and veterans of the North African campaign, raised the Fighting France flag in midtown New York, and set up recruiting and souvenir booths in the lobby of the Hollywood Theatre. In addition, the Office of War Information sent a report on the festivities around the world. The film even got a vote of approval from General Charles deGaulle, who requested that it be shown as soon as possible in London and the recently liberated French colonies.

Many of the reviews created a festive atmosphere to match the premiere, but contrary to legend, they were not unanimous raves. The most positive notices were those in the trade press, which responded favorably to the film's box-office potential. They emphasized a theme that would run throughout the notices, the lucky timing that made *Casablanca* the most topical title of the year.

The Hollywood Reporter's review begins, "Here is a drama that lifts you right out of your seat. That Warners had a lucky break in the progress of world events that put the name of Casablanca on everyone's lips is the answer to the surefire box-office smash the Hal B. Wallis production will enjoy." The *Daily Variety* review has a similar opening: "By a curious quirk of fortune, history making caught up to this picture set against a background of French Morocco, and its timeliness assures big box-office reception." A later *Variety* rave begins, "*Casablanca* will take the b.o.'s of America just as swiftly and certainly as the AEF took North Africa."

THE
FAMILY CIRCLE

JANUARY 29, 1943   VOL. 22   NO. 5

YOUR SOLDIER IS PROBABLY HEALTHIER ... in the Army than he would be at home, at Boyestown Steel demonstrates in its article. Above, Private Russell Green enjoys the kindly ministrations of Lieutenant Regina Switon in an Iceland hospital

HUMPHREY BOGART and INGRID BERGMAN ... are the love interest in 'Casablanca,' which our reviewer says is the kind of movie they always hope he won't let children see

BABIES ... are a subject that Uncle Sam can and gladly will give considerable attention to, as he has time, too, in Mrs. Norman's article

WARNER BROS. INTERNATIONAL NEWS BULLETIN

SPECIAL ISSUE

Dec. 1, 1942

WARNERS does it AGAIN!

November 27, 1942

« REVIEWS »

"Casablanca"

with Humphrey Bogart, Ingrid Bergman, Paul Henreid

Warners   102 Mins.

SMASHING MELODRAMA OF TIMELY IMPORT SHOULD CLICK HEAVILY AT BOX-OFFICES EVERYWHERE.

Casablanca! A magic word, that. A word that will open theater doors wide and keep them open. For the movement of humanity into houses where this Warner film is played will be constant and heavy. Yes, Casablanca is a word that piques the interest and stirs the imagination. The lightning developments in the North African theater of war have brought that name vividly into the consciousness of America. As a result this Warner picture should have the impact of a bombshell on film audiences of the country. The film's timeliness is its most priceless virtue. It is difficult to see how exhibitors can fail to clean up on so screaming a subject.

The entire action of the picture transpires in the French Moroccan city which in recent days has bulked so prominently in the news out of Africa. The film is an exciting and suspense-laden melodrama of Nazi intrigue. The events in the picture are so close to fact as to give "Casablanca" a fascination that is irresistible. Whirled about in the maelstrom of action are Humphrey Bogart, Ingrid Bergman and Paul Henreid. Bogart is an American with a shady past who operates a cafe and gambling joint peopled by a strange collection of characters.

Miss Bergman is his one-time love, now married to Henreid, a Czech whose work as head of the European underground has placed a price on his head. Bogart and Miss Bergman take up their romance where they left off. For a long time the man is torn between love and a sense of duty. After a lot of romantic torture Bogart turns sacrificial and makes it possible for Miss Bergman to get safely out of the country with her husband, who needs her moral aid to carry on his noble work in behalf of freedom.

The story, which deals heavily with the operation of the black market in Casablanca, has been skillfully contrived by Julius J. and Philip G. Epstein and Howard Koch from a play by Murray Burnett and Joan Alison. Their script has been directed by Michael Curtiz with a fine flow of movement and a punch that make "Casablanca" extremely gripping entertainment. The film, a Hal Wallis production, has been produced with high regard for showmanship and photographed by Arthur Edeson in highly commendable fashion. Max Steiner's music is a definite asset to the film. Bogart, Miss Bergman and Henreid perform capitally. Their acting points up beautifully the human drama of the story. Claude Rains does a swell job as a French officer who turns against...

siness with Warners' CASABLAN...

Both critical and popular reaction to CASABLANCA gave the Warner Bros. Publicity Department something to cheer about, as demonstrated in the two-page magazine ad (above), the "Variety" (far left) review reprinted in the film's press kit, and the other press kit pages (near left and above, right). "The Film Daily" review (right) was typical of the glowing notices the picture received in the trades, while the "Family Circle" cover (above, left) was one of many magazine covers and articles that helped spread the word about the season's biggest release .

Of the daily reviewers, Bosley Crowther's *New York Times* notice was probably the most encouraging: "The Warners here have a picture which makes the spine tingle and the heart take a leap. For once more, as in recent Bogart pictures, they have turned the incisive trick of draping a tender love story within the folds of a tight topical theme."

Howard Barnes of the *New York Herald Tribune* noted the topicality, too, but made sure readers knew this was not the film's only attraction: "Good writing, a brilliant cast and artful direction add up here to a superior show, as well as a significant document….*Casablanca* happens to be timely. It also happens to be an excellent film."

But a later review in the *Trib*, though generally favorable, points to the dismissive attitude some of the more "serious" film critics would take toward the picture. The unsigned notice describes the plot as "melodrama with a capital 'M'" and refers to the love story as "moving if at times slushy." In fact, a closer look at Crowther's review reveals another theme running through the film's criticism in the consumer press: yes, it was thrilling entertainment, but it was designed to be that way. Even the film's staunchest supporters among the New York critics saw it as a product, a commodity produced by one of the most successful film factories in the world. And, as such, they ranked it lower than the more artistic pictures of maverick directors like Orson Welles and John Ford.

The most discouraging notices came from the weekly and monthly press. Phillip Hartung in *Commonweal* thought *Casablanca* was entertaining, but its failure to reach the level of "sin and local color of *Algiers*" kept it from being a first-rate film. David Lardner of *The New Yorker* may have been the only reviewer to consider the story's timeliness a disadvantage: "Even though the armed forces might be said to have taken some of the play away

The cover of the "Warner Club News," Warner Bros.' in-house magazine, heralded all of the studio's Oscar winners for 1943, including AIR FORCE and PRINCESS O'ROURKE, but gave primary emphasis to the studio's surprise winner for Best Picture. Jack Warner is pictured top row, center.

from them, Warner Brothers have gone right ahead and released a film called *Casablanca*." He also dismissed the film lightly, stating that it was "not quite up to *Across the Pacific*, Bogart's last spyfest, [but] is nevertheless pretty tolerable…."

The most acerbic of all the reviewers was James Agee of *The Nation*. He did not mention the film until a February 1943 column in which he wondered about the fact that *Casablanca* was "working up a rather serious reputation as a fine melodrama." For all the enjoyment he had gotten out of the film and Ingrid Bergman's performance, Agee thought the writing was a bit obvious, particularly many of Claude Rains's lines. In addition, he called Michael Curtiz's direction overdone: "Curtiz still has a twenties director's correct feeling that everything, including the camera, should move; but the camera should move for purposes other than those of a nautch-dancer."

Yet, even the most negative reviews could not deny the film's virtues as entertainment. In addition, almost all the critics commented favorably on Bogart, Bergman, and Dooley Wilson (though Agee had to admit that he could not remember Wilson's name). In addition, almost all of them noted the one scene that never failed to move audiences: the scene in which the singing of "*La Marseillaise*" drowns out the Germans' rendition of "*Wacht am Rhein*."

With the critical fraternity so quick to dismiss *Casablanca* as enjoyable but empty, it is little wonder that the picture was barely mentioned in the voting for the New York Film Critics Awards. Bogart came in a distant second to Cagney in *Yankee Doodle Dandy*; Ingrid Bergman got only one vote in a wide Best Actress field dominated by Agnes Moorehead in *The Magnificent Ambersons*; and Michael Curtiz received but a single vote in the

Best Director competition won by John Farrow for *Wake Island*. Worse yet, *Casablanca* didn't get a single nomination for Best Film, an award that went to Noel Coward's English Navy saga, *In Which We Serve*.

Warner Bros. could content itself with the rewards it was reaping at the box office. The combination of a timely title and tremendous word of mouth attracted SRO crowds in New York. *Variety* predicted that the first week's receipts would reach $37,000 (at a top price of $1.25 per ticket), a new house record for the Hollywood Theatre. Within ten weeks, *Casablanca* had grossed $255,000 at that theater alone.

Just as the picture opened in Los Angeles and other U.S. cities on January 23, 1943, news broke about a summit meeting at which Franklin Roosevelt and Winston Churchill were planning the invasion of Europe. Their

Writer Howard Koch is called to the stage of Grauman's Chinese Theatre to receive his award for Best Screenplay. The small crowd was typical of early Oscar ceremonies, before the presentations became a national obsession on television.

meeting place? Casablanca, of course. This coincidence helped the picture bring in $3.7 million on its initial release, a solid profit on its final cost of approximately $950,000.

Because of its release pattern, *Casablanca* was listed as a 1943 film by the Academy of Motion Picture Arts and Sciences, and those awards would not be voted on until the beginning of 1944. By that time, the picture's initial release had essentially played out, but its popularity led to eight Oscar nominations: Best Picture, Actor (Bogart), Supporting Actor (Rains), Director, Screenplay, Cinematography, Score, and Editing. Bergman was nominated for Best Actress, but for playing Maria in *For Whom the Bell Tolls*. The other actors, along with Art Director Carl Jules Weyl, were bypassed, and because there were no awards for makeup or costuming at the time, Perc Westmore and Orry-Kelly were not eligible for nominations.

Casablanca was not favored to win. Bogart fully expected the Best Actor Oscar to go to Paul Lukas, who was repeating his stage performance in *Watch on the Rhine*. Bogie even planned to vote for Lukas himself.

Casablanca's competition for Best Picture seemed formidable at the time, though none of the films would challenge it now as a classic. Also up for the award were *For Whom the Bell Tolls*; *Heaven Can Wait*; *The Human Comedy*; *In Which We Serve*, which had not opened in Los Angeles until 1943; *Madame Curie*; *The More the Merrier*; *The Ox-Bow Incident*, which had beaten out *Casablanca* for the National Board of Review's Best Picture award; *The Song of Bernadette*; and *Watch on the Rhine*, which had won the New York Film Critics Award for Best Picture of 1943.

Of these, the odds-on favorite was *The Song of Bernadette*. The 20th Century–Fox religious drama about a young girl's vision of the Virgin Mary in nineteenth-century France was considered the prestige picture of the season and had garnered twelve nominations, the most that year. In addition, it was one of the most recent releases in contention: even in 1943 that was considered an advantage.

On March 2, 1944, Hollywood's finest gathered at Grauman's Chinese Theatre to celebrate the results of the voting. There were no surprised reactions when Dinah Shore presented the Best Scoring Oscar to Alfred Newman for *The Song of Bernadette* rather than to Max Steiner for *Casablanca*; Best Editing went to another Warner Bros. film, *Air Force*; and Rosalind Russell announced that *The Song of Bernadette* had won Best Cinematography. In addition, the Fox picture picked up the award for Interior Decoration.

Jack Warner accepts *CASABLANCA*'s Oscar for Best Picture. His decision to claim the award himself rather than accord that honor to Hal Wallis would finalize a rift with the producer that would lead Wallis to defect to Paramount Studios within a few months.

Then came the first upset of the evening. Novelist James Hilton announced the winner of the Best Screenplay award; *Casablanca* beat out *The Song of Bernadette*. Even though by this time nobody was certain who had written what—and there were four writers uncredited—Julius and Philip Epstein and Howard Koch were happy, if amazed, to accept the honor. The second surprise came when the Best Director award went to Michael Curtiz, who had not even prepared an acceptance speech. On reaching the stage, he launched into a priceless bit of garbled English: "So many times I have a speech ready, but no dice. Always a bridesmaid, never a mother."

As expected, Claude Rains lost Best Supporting Actor to Charles Coburn for *The More the Merrier*, and Humphrey Bogart lost Best Actor to Paul Lukas. Ingrid Bergman even forfeited the hotly contested race for Best Actress to Jennifer Jones in *The Song of Bernadette*.

But the big award of the evening brought the night's third shock. *Casablanca* beat the competition. When the winner was announced, there was a gasp before the audience broke into applause, and Jack Warner bounded to the podium. The film's real producer, Hal Wallis, was somewhat miffed to see Warner take credit for the film, but could console himself with winning the Irving G. Thalberg Memorial Award, his second, in recognition of outstanding work as a producer.

Daily Variety had a simple explanation of how *Casablanca* had worked its upset victory. Because the film had gone into release over a year before the voting, it had been seen by almost all of the voters—including the extras, who were allowed to cast ballots for Best Picture at the time. *The Song of Bernadette*, however, was still playing road-show engagements at higher prices, making it difficult for many Academy members, particularly the extras, to see the picture. And Academy members are honor-bound to vote only for achievements they have seen.

With *Casablanca*'s success at the box office and the Academy Awards, everybody should have been happy. At least, that would have been the reaction to such good fortune anywhere else in the world. But Hollywood is not anywhere else.

Hal Wallis's move into independent production may have brought him a great deal of satisfaction—and some great films—but it had not done anything to lessen the ill feelings between him and Jack Warner. Their relationship deteriorated after an interview with Wallis appeared in the *Los Angeles Daily News* on November 23, 1943. The article did not contain a single mention of Jack Warner.

Warner was furious, as documented by correspondence in Rudy Behlmer's excellent *Inside Warner Bros.* On November 28, he wired Wallis to complain about the article and raged that he would not allow him to take all the credit for his films at the studio: "I happened to be one who saw these stories, read plays, bought and turned them over to you. You could have at least said so, and I want to be accredited accordingly. You certainly have changed and unnecessarily so."

Wallis tried to smooth things over by assuring Warner he had indeed been mentioned during the interview, but the writer had omitted the references. That just added oil to the fires. Warner wired Publicity and Advertising Director Charles Einfeld to inform him that he would "definitely take legal action if this isn't stopped. Want you inform all producers diplomatically in giving stories or interviews that I shall be definitely accredited as executive producer or in charge of production. Sick, tired everyone taking all credit and I become small boy and doing most of work…." Warner was far from diplomatic with Wallis, however, repeating his threats to take legal action.

There were no further conflicts until War-

ner accepted the *Casablanca* Oscar. Although Wallis assured Edwin Schallert of *The Los Angeles Times*, which had run an item stating that Wallis was angry at Warner over the incident, that there was no rivalry between the two, Wallis began looking for a way to leave Warner Bros. Within the month he had freed himself and was ready to move onto a new affiliation, this time with Paramount, where he would remain for two decades.

On the advice of his brother Harry, Jack Warner rarely talked of Wallis after that. When he wrote his memoirs in 1965, he deliberately downplayed the producer's role in the Warners success story. Two years later, Warner sold off his share in the studio. Warners threw him a gala party on the set of *Camelot*, and most of the people whose careers had been touched by Jack Warner attended, including Hal Wallis.

By then, of course, Wallis could afford to be generous. His record as an independent producer continued undiminished after he left Warners. Among the stars whose careers he fostered were Kirk Douglas, Burt Lancaster, Lizabeth Scott, Dean Martin and Jerry Lewis, Shirley MacLaine, Charlton Heston, Shirley Booth, Anna Magnani, Elvis Presley, Geraldine Page,

Warner Bros. goes to the Academy Awards: (Left to right) director Lloyd Bacon, Jack Warner, writer Emil Ludwig, Hal Wallis, and producer-director Mervyn LeRoy.

Genevieve Bujold, and Richard Thomas. His later credits include *The Strange Love of Martha Ivers*; *Sorry, Wrong Number*; *The Furies*; *Come Back, Little Sheba*; *The Rose Tattoo*; *Gunfight at the O.K. Corral*; *King Creole*; *Summer and Smoke*; *Becket*; *True Grit*; *Anne of the Thousand Days*; *Mary Queen of Scots*; and *Rooster Cogburn*.

Casablanca's success turned Humphrey Bogart into one of the screen's greatest lovers, and nobody was more surprised than Bogart himself. Maintaining the cynical, self-deprecating image he had cultivated in the press, he told reporters, "I didn't do anything I've never done before. But when the camera moves in on that Bergman's face, and she's saying she loves you, it would make anybody look romantic."

Off-screen, Humphrey Bogart spent much of his time during CASABLANCA's shooting trying to mollify jealous wife Mayo Methot (top, right), who was convinced he was having an affair with Ingrid Bergman. A year later, he would give her some cause for jealousy, when he fell in love with his leading lady in TO HAVE AND HAVE NOT, Lauren Bacall (right, standing and below, right).

Casablanca put Bogart on top at Warner Bros. There would still be some less-than-perfect assignments, but on the whole during the forties, he fared better than any other male star there. He followed *Casablanca* with *To Have and Have Not*, *The Big Sleep*, *Dark Passage*, *The Treasure of the Sierra Madre*, and *Key Largo*, the last two with his favorite director, John Huston.

The image that made him a star was that of the loner shrouded in a haze of liquor and cigarette smoke, the man whose isolation stemmed either from romantic loss or the shattering of ideals in some long-ago youth. On-screen, he explored variations on cynical detatchment. Off-screen, he carefully projected the image of the sardonic iconoclast. He was the peg for many a reporter's favorite drunk story, a situation he helped by provoking more than a few barroom brawls himself.

During this period, he found the wife who would stay with him for the rest of his days. Mayo Methot may have been consumed with unwarranted jealousy during the filming of *Casablanca*, but when Bogie met his co-star in *To Have and Have Not*, a husky-voiced nineteen-year-old model named Lauren Bacall, Sluggy's fears became justified. As Bogart and Bacall worked together, they found themselves increasingly drawn to each other. And nobody watching the film could deny the amazing chemistry between the stars. By the time Warners re-teamed them for *The Big Sleep*, the Battling Bogarts had become history, and Bogie and his Baby were the new sweethearts of the gossip columns.

In 1947, Bogart, like so many other actors at the time, set up his own production company, Santana. Within two years, he had taken the company to another studio, Columbia, where he scored successes in *Knock on Any Door* and one of his best films, *In a Lonely Place*. The latter depicted another of his mentally disturbed loners, a type he would play again in *The Caine Mutiny* and *The Desperate Hours*.

Working as a free agent also brought

Bogart one of his most popular films, *The African Queen*. The picture was shot on location in the Congo for director John Huston and independent producer Sam Spiegel and released through United Artists. Teamed with Katharine Hepburn, Bogie was at his most playful, helping create another memorable romantic pairing to rank with his work opposite Ingrid Bergman and Lauren Bacall. He also was at his most grizzled. Charlie Allnut, the hard-drinking captain of a cargo boat chugging up and down the Ulanga-Bora, was a Rick Blaine who had been left out in the rain too long. The performance was popular enough to win Bogart his only Oscar.

Hit followed hit for Bogie in the fifties. He played against type as the sophisticated business tycoon who falls for Audrey Hepburn in *Sabrina*, romped through a black comedy about escaped convicts in *We're No Angels*, and made an impassioned plea to clean up the boxing game in *The Harder They Fall*. He was

Bogie and Walter Huston in John Huston's THE TREASURE OF THE SIERRA MADRE. As the paranoid loner Fred C. Dobbs, Bogart showed the dark side of the rugged individualists he had played in such hits as THE MALTESE FALCON and CASABLANCA.

preparing his fifth film with Bacall—an adaptation of J. P. Marquand's Washington-set comedy *Melville Goodwin, U.S.A.*—when a persistent cough turned out to be lung cancer. Humphrey Bogart died in 1957 at the age of fifty-eight. He was still at the height of his career but would miss the chance to witness his transformation into a cultural icon. He probably would have been amused.

Casablanca's success took Ingrid Bergman by surprise, too. She had been so frustrated at the lack of a completed script and so distracted by her interest in *For Whom the Bell Tolls*, that she could not see the merits of what would one day rank as her most popular film. In fact, she only saw *Casablanca* once during its initial release.

In the seventies, she was asked to lecture on the picture at the British Film Institute. Not knowing what to say, she did not prepare any remarks. Instead, she decided to watch the film with the audience and then answer questions. After three decades, *Casablanca* was a revelation to her. She had never realized how well it worked. When she got to the lectern, her opening comment, "What a good movie that was!" brought down the house.

Even if Bergman did not originally appreciate the merits of *Casablanca*, she clearly reaped the rewards. Although she had expected *For Whom the Bell Tolls* to make her a box-office name, it was *Casablanca* that did the trick, making her the third-most-popular female star in a 1943 poll.

As a result, she was in line for the best roles Hollywood had to offer. When Hedy Lamarr turned down *Gaslight*, Bergman got the part and won her first Oscar. Lamarr also turned down *Saratoga Trunk*, giving Bergman another box-office winner and a chance to work again with Gary Cooper. She won the New

The success of CASABLANCA helped Ingrid Bergman land two of the best women's roles of the 1940s: the tormented young wife in GASLIGHT (opposite, with Charles Boyer) which brought Bergman her first Oscar for Best Actress, and the saucy courtesan in Warners' adaptation of Edna Ferber's SARATOGA TRUNK (above, with Gary Cooper).

York Film Critics Award for two 1945 releases: *The Bells of St. Mary's* and her first Alfred Hitchcock film, *Spellbound*. Afterward, she went on to another Hitchcock hit, *Notorious*, which reunited her with Claude Rains and marked her first teaming with Cary Grant.

Bergman's contract with David O. Selznick ended in 1947, leaving her free to develop her own projects. High on the list was a role she had dreamed of for years, Joan of Arc. She became the first Tony Award winner for Best Actress for her Broadway appearance in Maxwell Anderson's *Joan of Lorraine*, and brought the character back to Hollywood for Walter Wanger's epic production *Joan of Arc*.

But in 1949, Bergman did something no other Hollywood star would have dared. She traveled to Italy to work for peanuts in a film directed by Roberto Rossellini, one of the Neorealist directors whose work was finding support in art-film houses. On the set a romance developed, which everyone tried to keep quiet—until she discovered she was pregnant.

Bergman had certainly played her share of bad girls—the amoral party girl in *Notorious*, the streetwalker in *Arch of Triumph*, the courtesan in *Saratoga Trunk*—but it was the saintly roles that had formed her public image and that made the scandal doubly shocking. When word got out that this respectable married woman had deserted husband and child for another man, the American public felt betrayed.

Joan of Arc was released after the scandal broke, by which time the casting seemed like a dirty joke. The picture flopped, and Bergman and Rossellini's film, *Stromboli*, did even worse. She was even denounced from the floor of the U.S. Congress. Her Hollywood career was over.

Through the next several years, Bergman worked almost entirely in Italy. It was a period of critical disfavor for both her and her new Italian husband, though in recent years their

films together—*Europa '51, Viaggio in Italia, Joan at the Stake*, and *Angst*—have been reevaluated as minor masterpieces.

By 1957, however, Rossellini's continental approach to wedded bliss proved too much for Bergman. He had gone off to India to produce a ten-part documentary for Italian television and returned with one of that country's leading screenwriters as his pregnant mistress, a situation that led Bergman to seek an annulment.

The American public was ready to welcome her back, and 20th Century–Fox offered her the plum role of an escaped mental patient who might or might not be the last surviving member of the Russian royal family. *Anastasia* was shot on location in Europe and was scheduled for a U.S. release to qualify for the 1956 Oscars.

Many people were already prepared to forgive and forget, and their numbers increased when Broadway columnist and television host Ed Sullivan held a poll to find out if people thought Bergman had paid for her sins. The move was so tasteless that it actually increased public support for the actress.

Bergman returned in triumph, winning solid reviews for *Anastasia* along with the New York Film Critics Award and her second Oscar. She moved into television with an Emmy-winning performance in *The Turn of the Screw* and suddenly found herself acclaimed as one of the world's great actresses.

ABOVE: Bergman was eager to work with Italian director Roberto Rossellini, who had introduced the world to Neorealism with OPEN CITY in 1945, but STROMBOLI (above, with unidentified child) and their on-set affair almost destroyed her career. Bergman would return to favor after their divorce, making her comeback in ANASTASIA in 1956.
BELOW: Paul Henreid gave one of his best performances as the concentration-camp victim who returns to childhood love Bette Davis in DECEPTION, but it was too little, too late.

The star moved into character leads in the sixties and, though she had some trouble finding the best roles on film, continued to prove a popular attraction on stage and television. A cameo performance in the all-star *Murder on the Orient Express* brought her a third Oscar, this time for Best Supporting Actress, in 1974.

Still more triumphs were ahead. In 1978, she joined forces for the only time with fellow-Swede Ingmar Bergman to appear opposite Liv Ullman in *Autumn Sonata*. Although gossip spread that her role as a world-famous concert pianist called to account for neglecting her children was loosely based on her own life, none could deny the power of her performance. The film brought her a third New York Film Critics Award and another Oscar nomination.

The film's completion also brought sad news. Bergman was suffering from cancer and, because of the strain of chemotherapy, had decided to stop making movies. But she allowed herself to be talked into one more project.

In 1982, already in great pain, she accepted the role of Israeli Prime Minister Golda Meir in the independently produced television miniseries *A Woman Called Golda*. The location shoot was extremely uncomfortable, but she turned in a glowing performance, particularly in the scene in which Meir learns she has leukemia. The actress's delivery

of the line "Well, I'm sixty-six. How long can I expect to live anyway?" was so moving, cameraman Alan Greenberg could not watch it. On August 28, 1982, only two months after completing *Golda*, she died. Bergman's performance won her a posthumous Emmy for Best Actress in a Movie or Miniseries.

A s Paul Henreid had feared, *Casablanca* did not help his career. Though it is hard to determine exactly what kept the actor from rising to the top rank of stars, certainly his secondary role as Victor Laszlo stopped the career momentum created by his appearances in *Joan of Paris* and *Now, Voyager*.

He has often stated that his shared contract with Warners and RKO kept him from getting the buildup he needed. There were two other mitigating factors, as well. Hal Wallis's departure from Warner Bros. was accompanied by a significant drop in the quality of the studio's films. There were still some good pictures ahead—particularly such Jerry Wald productions as *Mildred Pierce*, *Johnny Belinda*, *Key Largo*, and *Humoresque*—but none of them had roles for Henreid. Other producers gave him good parts in *Between Two Worlds*, *In Our Time*, and *Of Human Bondage*, but the final films were disappointing on all counts. He also re-teamed with Bette Davis, his most popular co-star, for *Deception*, but though the picture did well, it has never been considered one of her best vehicles.

It has been suggested that Henreid was a victim of the new interest in realism that followed World War II. The mold in which he had been cast, the continental lover, was on the way out. There still was room for the type at MGM, one of Hollywood's last glamour hold-outs, but that studio had its own Latin lovers, Ricardo Montalban and Fernando Lamas.

By the fifties, Henreid moved into supporting roles, while also branching out into directing and production. In fact, his third reunion with Bette Davis put them on opposite sides of the camera when he directed her in 1964's *Dead Ringer*. Henreid made his last professional

Three examples of how
CASABLANCA has become part
of popular culture.

Son of Casablanca

Director Michael Curtiz got to take a stab at re-creating the magic of *Casablanca* when he took on another Free French vs. Vichy story, *Passage to Marseilles*, in 1944. Bogart was cast in the leading role as an anti-fascist journalist sentenced to Devil's Island. He leads an escape so he can fight with the Allies. The plot did not center on his move into action; instead, Bogart provided the example for his fellow escapees, who ended up joining him in a desperate stand against the Germans in the final reel.

Fleshing out the cast were several other actors from *Casablanca*: Claude Rains, Sydney Greenstreet, Peter Lorre, Helmut Dantine, and even Corinna Mura. In addition, the film featured three players who had been under consideration for *Casablanca* but did not make the cast: Michelle Morgan—finally getting to play love scenes with Bogie—Phillip Dorn, and George Tobias.

Warners even held up release hoping that an Allied landing in the south of France would provide the same boost to ticket sales that the invasion of North Africa had given to *Casablanca*. But the Allies landed in Normandy instead. The film was still a success, but not on the same scale as its predecessor.

Michelle Morgan (above) finally got to work with Humphrey Bogart in PASSAGE TO MARSEILLES. The film also reunited Bogart with (below, left to right, with Victor Francen) Sydney Greenstreet, Claude Rains, and Peter Lorre.

appearance in 1977 in *Exorcist II: The Heretic*, a box-office disaster unjustly labeled one of the worst films ever made. He currently lives in the Hollywood area, maintaining a presence at revivals of his most famous films, where he still delights fans by repeating his double-cigarette trick from *Now, Voyager* and telling stories about the filming of *Casablanca*.

Almost everybody else from *Casablanca*'s cast profited from their association with the surprise hit. But for actors like Claude Rains, Sydney Greenstreet, and Peter Lorre, who were already firmly ensconced in the studio system, the film was not critical in advancing their careers. Conrad Veidt did not live long enough to enjoy the picture's success. He would complete only one more film—*Above Suspicion*, another war story, in which he menaced U.S. secret agent Joan Crawford—before dying at the age of fifty, just as *Casablanca* was going into general release.

None of the other supporting players scored as solidly with fans as Dooley Wilson. After the film went into release, he got a call from Warner Bros. to come pick up his fan mail. He was receiving about five thousand letters a week, more than box office idol Clark Gable got at MGM.

Hollywood, however, did not know what to do with a black singer-actor who was pushing sixty. Though "As Time Goes By" was enjoying a resurgence of popularity, a snafu with the Musicians Union kept Wilson from making his own recording (these were the days before soundtrack albums were issued). Wilson followed *Casablanca* with a good-sized supporting role in the all-black musical *Stormy Weather*, but fans were disappointed at his smaller part in *Higher and Higher*, Frank Sinatra's first starring vehicle.

After a few more stereotyped roles, Wilson returned to New York and nightclub work. His first club engagement brought a surprise. When Wilson arrived, the manager asked him where he wanted his piano. Wilson had to explain that his playing had been dubbed in *Casa-*

TOP AND RIGHT: Hal Wallis tried to copy CASABLANCA with ROPE OF SAND in 1949. Co-starring with Burt Lancaster were Claude Rains, Paul Henreid, and Peter Lorre. ABOVE, BOTTOM: Another Warners imitation of CASABLANCA, THE CONSPIRATORS (1944), featured such CASABLANCA players as Henreid, Sydney Greenstreet, and Lorre, along with Hedy Lamarr.

blanca, and all that he was prepared to do in the show was sing.

In 1944, Wilson opened on Broadway with a supporting role as an escaped slave in the Harold Arlen musical *Bloomer Girl*. He won strong notices and solid applause for his renditions of "The Eagle and Me" and "I Got a Song." He would continue appearing in revivals of the show until his death in 1953.

With *Casablanca*'s success, it was only natural that Warner Bros. should consider a sequel. The first announcement came shortly after the film opened nationally. The project was called *Brazzaville* and presumably would have dealt with Rick and Renault's adventures together after they joined the Free French garrison there. Ideally, the film also would have featured the return of Ingrid Bergman as Ilsa.

Though there is no script or outline for *Brazzaville* on file, there is a ten-page synopsis of an untitled sequel written by Frederick Stephani. In this version, Renault and Rick return to the café after seeing off the Laszlos. There, a group of German officers demands Rick's arrest. Knowing the Allied invasion is imminent, Renault stalls them—an impressive job as the invasion took place a year after the original film's action; in the sequel, however, the gap is only six hours.

With the Allies in control of Casablanca, Rick is something of a local hero. At the request of the Allies, he goes undercover to Tangiers to ferret out a sabotage ring responsible for the sinking of U.S. ships carrying war supplies to Russia and Turkey. Rick leaves just before Ilsa, now conveniently widowed, returns to Casablanca looking for him.

In Tangiers, Rick worms his way into the German consulate by posing as a dealer in black-market visas. He also wins the affections of a female German spy named Maria. As he is about to get the goods on the spies, however, Ilsa shows up, triggering a crisis that is resolved when Maria sacrifices her life to save Rick. The sabotage ring is destroyed, and Rick and Ilsa sail off happily for America.

Needless to say, this story was not met with boundless enthusiasm at Warner Bros. Hal Wallis sent it around to various writers for comments. The one response on file at the University of Southern California comes from Frederick Faust, better known to western fans by his pen name, Max Brand.

He correctly points out that by setting the action after the liberation of Casablanca and making Rick an Allied agent, the proposed sequel robbed him of his special position as an outsider. Faust also felt that the shift of locale away from Casablanca would be a disappointment to

Years after losing the role to Dooley Wilson, Clarence Muse (left) got to play Sam in the 1955 television series based on CASABLANCA. Charles McGraw (right) was Rick.

fans, who probably would come to the film for another dose of the atmosphere created in the original.

With a stronger sense of time, Faust suggests centering the action around the upcoming Allied landing, with Rick working surreptitiously to help pave the way. The triangle involving Rick, Ilsa, and the German spy could be maintained, with an emphasis on Rick's desire to be with Ilsa while duty demands he maintain his connection with the other woman. With the arrival of the Allies at the end, Rick would realize that he was still an outcast (because of the unnamed crime that forced him to leave the U.S. in the first place) and that it was time to move on. "If a happy ending is wanted," Faust concluded, "he is able to take Ilsa with him."

Faust's suggestions had a lot more potential for success than the earlier outline, but it was not to be. The existence of a sequel to *Casablanca* would be decided, not by anyone at Warner Bros., but by David O. Selznick. These were the days when, for the most part, sequels were considered to be second-rate productions. As a result, Selznick came to the conclusion that another *Casablanca* would not necessarily be in Ingrid Bergman's best interests. On April 17, 1943, a New York gossip columnist reported that the independent producer had informed Warners that Bergman would not be available for a sequel. The studio briefly considered teaming Bogart with Geraldine Fitzgerald for a sequel without Ilsa, but *Casablanca* without Ingrid Bergman just did not have the same magic.

Even without a sequel, however, *Casablanca* would live on through revivals and reincarnations in other media. On April 26, 1943, Humphrey Bogart, Ingrid Bergman, and Paul Henreid recreated their roles on CBS radio's "Screenguild Players." This was fairly common practice at the time. There were numerous such radio shows to allow the studios to get a little extra publicity for their films and a little extra exposure for their stars. The real upsurge in *Casablanca's* popularity, though, would come with the arrival of television.

Warner Bros. was one of the first studios to embrace the medium, both by syndicating its films to local stations and by producing for television. The studio's initial entry into production was an anthology called "Warner Brothers Presents," consisting of alternating series adapted from three Warners films, *Cheyenne*, *Kings Row*, and *Casablanca*. (There had been a one-hour live dramatization on "The Phillip Morris Program" in 1953, but Warners would not allow any kinescopes to be saved.)

The series based on *Casablanca* debuted on ABC in September of 1955. Charles McGraw, a one-time RKO contractee who had been effective as the he-man star of *The Narrow Margin*, was Rick, with a supporting cast most notable for its connections to the original film. French actor Marcel Dalio was promoted from the croupier at Rick's Café to the post of Police Captain Renault. Heavyweight Dan Seymour had grown up from his status as "the young Sydney Greenstreet" to inherit the role of Ferrari. And Clarence Muse finally got to play Sam, the role he had lost to Dooley Wilson.

The television show was set after the film's action, with Rick and Renault fighting off such contemporary menaces as Communist spies. The series also featured a curious guest appearance by Anita Ekberg as a woman who might or might not have been Ilsa Laszlo. But none of this was enough to attract an audience. After a single season, "Casablanca" and "Kings Row" were cancelled, to be replaced by two westerns in the style of the anthology's only hit, "Cheyenne."

However, television would bring the original *Casablanca* to new generations of fans. The picture was among those sold into syndication in the early fifties, and it became a mainstay of local programmers. Its compact running time easily fit two-hour time slots (and many programmers have cut the film to fit slots of ninety minutes or less), while the continuing popularity of the stars and

Here's looking at who, kid? One of the guest stars on Warners' "Casablanca" series was Anita Ekberg, as a woman who could have been Ilsa Lund. Although the former Miss Sweden shared Ingrid Bergman's homeland, her image was far from the luminous purity Bergman radiated.

the story usually insures solid ratings. In fact, a 1977 *TV Guide* poll, more than two decades after the film first appeared on television, named *Casablanca* the most popular and frequently shown movie on television.

Most historians credit the Brattle Theatre, a revival house in Cambridge, Massachusetts, with starting the *Casablanca* cult. Beginning in the sixties, the theater's management booked the film for three weeks each year, and usually it was the best-attended offering of the season. The audience did not just watch the film. Many of them lived it, arriving in costume, complete with trench coats and snap-brim hats, and reciting Rick's dialogue with him. In fact, the film was so popular that the bar located beneath the theater changed its name to The Casablanca.

The film—and Bogart—eventually enjoyed an equal popularity among the French. Ironically, *Casablanca* bombed when it was shown in Paris after the war, mainly because of the way it depicted life under the German occupation. The French preferred their survival stories told in more metaphorical terms. *Gone With the Wind* was a huge hit in Paris after the war because the audience could see its own plight mirrored in Scarlett O'Hara's fight to build a better tomorrow during the days of the Civil War and Reconstruction.

And France was not the only country to resist *Casablanca* at first. The film was severely edited in Sweden and Germany, where Major Strasser and all references to the Nazis were cut entirely.

But over time, *Casablanca* and its star won a devoted following among the French. Bogie's characters, with their adherence to a personal moral code, had a powerful appeal in the land of existentialism. By 1959, he had risen to the level of international icon. In Jean-Luc Goddard's film *Breathless*, the linchpin

Producer David Wolper set out to create his own version of CASABLANCA, when he masterminded the 1983 series based on the film. Originally, David Soul (left) wanted to wear a moustache to make his Rick Blaine different from Humphrey Bogart's, and unlike Claude Rains, Hector Elizondo (right) played Captain Renault with a French accent.

film in the development of France's New Wave, the petty crook played by Jean-Paul Belmondo stops in front of a Bogart movie poster and tries to imitate his—and his generation's—idol.

Whenever anyone creates a list of the most popular films of all time, *Casablanca* always holds a place near the top. The American Film Institute, to celebrate its tenth anniversary in 1976, asked its members to vote on the best American films of all time. Though the voting was dominated by recent releases such as *One Flew Over the Cuckoo's Nest* and *Star Wars*, the top three films were *Gone With the Wind*, *Citizen Kane*, and *Casablanca*. By 1983, the film's stock had risen when, in the British Film Institute's fiftieth-anniversary poll of its members, *Casablanca* came out on top.

With the continuing popularity of *Casablanca*, it was only natural that television should take another stab at the story. In 1983, NBC unveiled a series set prior to the film's action, with David Soul, former star of the series "Here Come the Brides" and "Starsky & Hutch," as Rick, Hector Elizondo as Renault, Scatman Crothers as Sam, and future "goodfella" Ray Liotta as a decidedly more serious Sasha the bartender than the character played by Leonid Kinsky.

"None of us set out to do an imitation," noted Elizondo in a recent interview. "As I recall, the networks had to persuade David Soul, who has such integrity, not to wear a moustache. That's how far he wanted to be removed from the image of Bogart. We were going to do our own 'Casablanca.'

"The most thrilling part of it, besides being part of cinematic history, was that the set and many of the artifacts that we used were from the original production. So, there would be people walking through there, parades of people coming to see the set. People who had worked in the movie. My stand-in and his brother, they were in the original production as actors, when they were young men. And of course, it was very nostalgic for them to come to this set every day and see Casablanca all over again. Here it was 1983, and here they were being in an environment they had worked in in the '40s."

Despite solid production values and strong performances, lightning refused to strike twice. The series was cancelled after three weeks.

By the early 1980s, technicians had been working on a method of using computers to add color to black-and-white videotapes. To some, this idea was a sacrilege. To others, it was a sound investment. When cable-magnate R. E. "Ted" Turner acquired Warner Bros.'s pre-1950 films, he embarked on an ambitious pro-

gram of colorizing the classics from his library, starting with *Yankee Doodle Dandy* in 1986. The films would premiere on his Atlanta-based TBS SuperStation, then be available for syndication and home-video release: it was hoped they would be received as fresh product.

There was an outcry in the Hollywood community. With the Director's Guild taking the lead, a major protest was launched that even led to congressional hearings on the issue. Such luminaries as James Stewart, Woody Allen, Martin Scorsese, and Ginger Rogers stated their objections to colorization—calling it a vandalization comparable to painting a moustache on the Mona Lisa.

The result was the creation of the National Film Registry, a listing of films which were considered national treasures and could not be altered without an informative notice preceding the altered version. As was to be expected, *Casablanca* was among the first chosen for the Registry. In 1988, when Turner

Rick looked at Ilsa through brown eyes when Ted Turner ordered the colorization of CASABLANCA. Although many in the industry decried the film's new version, some critics actually liked it. And, like most other color-enhanced films, it did well in syndication.

PICTORIAL PREVIEW

"Casablanca" starring Humphrey Bogart — Ingrid Bergman — Paul Henreid

Images like those reproduced in the 1942 press kit have stayed with CASABLANCA's many fans for half a century, and many of them have had great popularity when reproduced as posters.

announced plans to colorize *Casablanca*, the Directors Guild complained again, but by that time the controversy had largely died down.

Colorization did indeed create new markets for the pictures, particularly in syndication. In addition, one prerequisite for the process was the creation of a pristine black-and-white negative, which often meant making new negatives for films that had not been restored in decades. This underlined the company's commitment to restoring and preserving the films in its library and demonstrated another benefit of colorization.

When the colorized *Casablanca* premiered on TBS Super-Station on November 9, 1988, it even got some favorable reviews from television critics, many of whom, by that time, felt the process was coming of age. (Later, it would provide one of the better jokes in *Gremlins 2: The New Batch*, in which the media/real-estate magnate played by John Glover—a character modeled on Donald Trump and Ted Turner—announced the telecast of *Casablanca*, "in full color and with a happy ending.")

Whatever one thought of the color choices for this new *Casablanca*, nothing could diminish the film's power with audiences, a power demonstrated not just by its popularity in theaters, on television, and on home video, but by the continued prominence of memorabilia associated with the picture.

Humphrey Bogart gave the poster industry its biggest boost in the early sixties. Just as young film fans were flocking to his movies, they also were decorating their walls with pictures of the star. And the most popular of all the Bogart posters were those depicting him as Rick Blaine.

Over the past few years, commerce in movie memorabilia has become a major business. In 1984, the Motion Picture Arts Gallery offered a poster from *Casablanca*'s Belgian release for $800. A year later, a billboard-sized poster from the original U.S. release was auctioned off for $5,000, only $400 less than the record set in 1980 by the poster for Walt Disney's 1925 *Alice in the Jungle*. Collectors Showcase, which made the sale after acquiring the poster in a collection that had not changed hands in forty years, also got $3,500 each for a smaller poster and a set of lobby cards.

In 1986, the car that drove Rick, Renault, and the Laszlos to the Casablanca airport was put on the auction block with an asking price of $35,000. Warner Bros. musician Lyle Ritz had acquired the Buick Limited convertible, stripped of all identifying insignia but complete with cigarette burns that may or may not have been made by Humphrey Bogart, in 1970 for $3,457.

Another vehicle used in the film, the Lockheed Electra 12A shown taking off at the end of *Casablanca*, was discovered dusting crops in 1987. It was purchased for use in the Great Movie Ride attraction at Disney World in Orlando, Florida.

The Marx Brothers Meet Casablanca

In 1946, the Marx Brothers set out to spoof international intrigue thrillers with *A Night in Casablanca*, all about a Nazi spy ring operating out of a North African hotel and nightclub. The film even featured Dan Seymour, who had played Rick's Arab bodyguard, Abdul.

Jack Warner ordered his lawyers to get the word "Casablanca" out of the title. All he got, however, was a string of vituperative letters from Groucho. The comic started by asking if the city now belonged exclusively to Warner Bros., then went on to wonder if Jack thought the average viewer could not tell the difference between Ingrid Bergman and Harpo Marx. Then, he accused the studio of a little title infringement of its own: "You probably have the right to use the name

LEFT TO RIGHT: Harpo, Groucho, and Chico Marx pose with a camel co-star from A NIGHT IN CASABLANCA, a spoof whose title roused the ire of Jack Warner and led to a string of accusatory, often quite hilarious, letters from Groucho.

Warner, but what about Brothers? Professionally, we were brothers long before you were."

Each time the lawyers wrote to Groucho about his film, trying to ascertain if the plot was stolen from *Casablanca*, he responded with ever-more-confusing synopses, including one in which, "Harpo marries a hotel detective; Chico operates an ostrich farm. Humphrey Bogart's girl, Bordello, spends her last years in a Bacall house."

Eventually, Warner surrendered. But Groucho had one more laugh on the studio head. When Warners announced the release of a Cole Porter biography entitled *Night and Day*, Groucho accused them of stealing the title from two Marx Brothers offerings: *A Night at the Opera* and *A Day at the Races*.

ABOVE: The tower glimpsed in the background of CASABLANCA's airport was available for rent in 1984. The problems of "three little people" got a contemporary spin when Woody Allen paid tribute to CASABLANCA in PLAY IT AGAIN, SAM. Diane Keaton (opposite, left) was the confused recipient of the film's famous climactic speech, while Jerry Lacey (below, right) was the ghost of Bogart.

But the most valued piece of *Casablanca* memorabilia is the piano on which Dooley Wilson pretended to play "As Time Goes By." It was put up for auction in 1988, at which time the Japanese trading firm of C. Itoh & Co. paid $154,000 for it. That offer represents the second-highest sum ever paid for a movie prop or costume. (The record was set that same year when an unnamed Canadian collector bid $165,000 to buy a pair of the ruby slippers from *The Wizard of Oz.*)

With *Casablanca*'s undiminished popularity over the years, Murray Burnett and Joan Allison saw one of their dreams come true—*Everybody Comes to Rick's* finally made it to the stage. Actually, there had been a stage production of the original play in Rhode Island for a five-night run in 1946, but Warners had stipulated in granting the rights that the playwrights were not to be credited in any way. Finally, after trying to regain some control of their original property in a failed lawsuit in the eighties, Burnett and Allison got Warner Bros. to grant them permission to have their original play staged.

In 1991, British producer Paul Elliott, the man behind the hit West End musical biography of Buddy Holly, *Buddy*, opened *Rick's Bar Casablanca* at the Whitehall Theatre in London. (The title was arrived at through a compromise with Warners after Elliott asked to call the play *Casablanca*.) Despite the presence of popular television actor Leslie Grantham, one of the stars of the popular British soap opera "Eastenders," the production ran only six weeks. But at least it allowed Burnett to remind people that his play had served as the film's basis and had provided a lot more than just the locale.

Casablanca hit the stage in another form in 1969 with Woody Allen's hit comedy *Play It Again, Sam*. The play, and the 1972 movie based on it, presents a humorous take on the powerful role a film like *Casablanca* can play in someone's life. The writer stars as Allen Felix, a recently divorced film buff whose fantasies are consumed with images from his favorite movie. He is even visited by a ghostly Bogart who serves as his advisor on life and love. When he temporarily falls in love with his best friend's wife (played by Diane Keaton), he sends her off with her husband by using Bogie's famous "hill of beans" speech on the bewildered woman, following it with, "I waited my whole life just to say it."

The film is one of the most frequent subjects of spoofs, take-offs, and homages in every medium. The first time Candice Bergen hosted "Saturday Night Live," she played Ilsa to John Belushi's Rick. The comedy series "227" did a mostly black version of the film, with Marla Gibbs as Ilsa, Hal Williams as Humphrey Bogart, and singer-songwriter Paul Williams as Sam. And the character Larry Mannitti played on Tom Selleck's "Magnum, P.I." series renamed himself Rick and spent one episode dressed in a white tuxedo in an effort to become his idol.

Chapter Seven

Here's LOOKING At You, KID

One of the characteristics that has kept Humphrey Bogart's acting alive to generations of fans is the fact that he does his most important work in little details which might escape the conscious eye on first viewing but that enrich the performance nonetheless. Note the slight sneer Bogie uses when telling Ugarte, "I am a little more impressed with you," a gesture that combines surprise that Lorre's character would commit murder to get the exit visas with disgust that the man would actually go so far. Later, when Ferrari offers to buy Sam's contract, Bogie sums up his character's feelings about his own politics by underplaying the liberal statement given him by Howard Koch, "I don't buy or sell human beings." By looking down as he says the line, Rick seems almost embarrassed, possibly by the memory of how hard he once fought to prevent the buying or selling of such a precious commodity as human life.

Bogart had a way of emptying himself in reaction to others. He does it during Annina's speech about sacrificing herself for her husband, just before he helps the two kids escape. And he does it again in the scene in his Casablanca apartment, when Ilsa tells him, "You'll have to think for both of us, for all of us."

Perhaps the finest of Bogart's screen moments occurs in the last scene at Rick's place, when Renault tries to arrest Victor for possession of the stolen visas. As Renault announces, "Victor Laszlo, you are under arrest on a charge of accessory to the murder of the couriers from whom those letters were stolen," the direction in the published script reads, *Ilsa and Laszlo are both caught completely off guard. They turn toward Rick. Horror is in Ilsa's eyes.* But that is not exactly what happens in the film. On screen, Ilsa moves automatically to her husband's side. The moment is visually reinforced by the blocking—the composition starts with Rick between her and Victor; her cross puts her on the other side of Rick, leaving him on the outside. And Rick is all too aware of the move. For Bogart, that moment brings the painful realization that he has made the right choice, that Ilsa belongs with Victor, and that, if she stays behind, she will regret it.

Ingrid Bergman has often told interviewers of her frustration over not knowing where the plot of *Casablanca* was going and the problem of finding a way to play her character "in between." She clearly found the solution.

The key can be seen in her reactions during two different musical moments in the film. On Ilsa's first appearance at Rick's Café, her behavior is furtive, almost hunted. To the rare viewer watching the film with no prior knowledge of the plot, her actions seem to be a natural result of her refugee status, the fear that she and her husband could be apprehended at any moment.

OPPOSITE: The purity Ingrid Bergman radiated in CASABLANCA and other films made her barely restrained passion for Rick Blaine even more striking. BELOW: Even during CASABLANCA's initial release, Warners treated it as an essential part of contemporary culture. BOTTOM: The film's strong visuals made it a natural for "comic-book" treatment in "Movie Show" magazine.

When Ilsa finally gets Sam to play "As Time Goes By," however, the real reason for her nervousness becomes apparent. As Sam sings, the film cuts to her reaction. She is transformed, almost fearfully, by the passion of the moment and her memory of what she shared with Rick. It is now clear that she has not been afraid of the Nazis, but of herself and her response to seeing Rick again.

The idea that passion is the basis of her feelings for Rick is reinforced by one scene during the Paris flashback. In the sequence set in Ilsa's apartment, which starts with her line "A franc for your thoughts," the actress chooses to play her character slightly drunk, mirroring physically the way her character has been emotionally swept away. And whether the staging of the scene's climactic embrace resulted from Bogie's decision to make Bergman come to him throughout the picture or someone else's choice, the fact that she initiates the kiss, moving up to meet Bogart's lips as they sit on the sofa, gives Ilsa's behavior a sense of reckless abandonment.

The kicker in the presentation of her relationship with Rick comes at the end of their late-night confrontation in his Casablanca apartment. After all the explanations have been made, and it appears that Rick and Ilsa will be together forever, she asks him if he will help Victor now, so that "he'll have his work, all that he's been living for." As Rick responds with, "All except one. He won't have you," Bergman buries her face on Bogart's shoulder, as if hiding some inner shame at the depth of her passion. It is a supremely romantic gesture in a supremely romantic film and one that clearly defines the nature of her feelings for Rick.

Ilsa's feelings for Laszlo are captured during the scene in which he leads the orchestra at Rick's in "*La Marseillaise*." In some of the best editing in the film, Owen Marks cuts between Victor and the others at the café pouring their

This publicity still, one of the most famous from the film, captures Ilsa's plight as a woman torn between two lovers. It also represents the subtler conflicts facing Captain Renault, caught between his friendship with Rick, his sympathy for the Laszlos, and his Nazi superiors.

hearts into the French national anthem. But in the midst of this, he also gives Ilsa two closeups. She isn't singing. She is gazing at Victor in a state approaching awe, an almost uncontrollable admiration for the man she has married. That look is repeated in the hotel-room scene later, when Victor tries to tell her that he understands about her relationship with Rick ("I know how it is to be lonely"). And the scene has been shot and cut to favor Bergman, to clarify the admiration at the base of her feelings for Victor.

In the airport scene, Ilsa is prepared to give in to her passion by running off with Rick. Instead, she finds herself facing a different man. Rick's self-sacrifice in sending her off with Victor for the good of the cause suddenly puts him in the same league as her husband. Rick becomes the perfect man for her, a fitting recipient for both her passion and her admiration. And at the moment she realizes that, she loses him.

Of all *Casablanca*'s cast, Paul Henreid has been most frequently criticized by fans and reviewers. People have complained that he does not have the passion of a great resistance leader, that he somehow unbalances the romantic triangle by not being fiery enough to deserve Ilsa.

Henreid's performance may be undervalued because of the unfortunate tendency among critics to view an actor's work not in terms of the script, but in terms of preconceived notions about the character type. Victor Laszlo is described as one of the most important figures in the resistance movement, and, as such, most viewers expect him to be the image of vitality and charisma. If that were all Henreid had to play, there would be no problem. Everything his critics say is lacking in his Victor can be found in his performance in *Joan of Paris*. But that character is not Victor Laszlo, and Victor's status as a resistance leader is not the only thing the script tells us about Laszlo.

Victor has been in and out of concentration camps. When he finally escaped, he was so ill that Ilsa had to cancel her plans to leave Paris with Rick to help her husband regain his health. And for the previous two years, the couple has been on the run, trying desperately to elude the Third Reich—hardly the best of circumstances under which to recuperate.

In Casablanca, Victor has a perilous path to tread. Although technically the city is ruled by Unoccupied France, it is still heavily under Nazi influence. One misstep could prevent Victor from getting to America, where he hopes to raise support for the underground fighters. Simply refusing to let Strasser sit at his table is an act of defiance that could cost him his freedom. Leading the orchestra in *"La Marseillaise"* to drown out the singing of the German officers is virtually an act of revolution.

The latter scene is undoubtedly Victor's strongest moment in the film. But even here, he is undermined by the fact that the orchestra needs Rick's permission to respond to Victor's request. For all the passion Henreid pours into the scene, it is Rick, not Victor, who comes off as the hero.

Because of the fine line Victor has to tread, Henreid chooses to emphasize the character's simplicity and quiet strength. Whether questioning his wife about her involvement with Rick, trying to win Rick over to the cause, or refusing to name names for Major Strasser, he takes a matter-of-fact approach in stark contrast to the behavior of others around him.

In the publicity shots taken for *Casablanca*, there are pictures of Henreid posed as if leading a political rally, though he never does anything of the sort in the picture. Had the scriptwriters allowed the audience to see Victor addressing the resistance meeting in Casablanca, it would at least have given Henreid a chance to present Victor as a leader. But even here, the facts in the script do not necessarily support such an image. When Strasser describes Victor's work in the resistance, he does

With no idea where Ilsa's heart lay—at least during the first seven weeks of shooting—Ingrid Bergman chose to play her as a woman torn between two different kinds of love: passion for Rick and admiration for her husband.

not speak of him as an organizer or a rabble-rouser, but as a writer. For all his importance to the movement, Victor's greatest contribution is not speaking in front of crowds, but putting words down on paper. That would make him a very different man from the one some people expect to see in *Casablanca*.

Beyond the given circumstances of Victor's past are the requirements of the film's present. For the romantic triangle and its resolution to work, the character has to provide a contrast to Rick. Ilsa must have something to choose between, not a Victor who offers everything she could possibly want and a Rick who could be her ideal if he would ever stop wallowing in the past. Part of the power of the film's conclusion lies in the knowledge that, for all Victor's virtues, Ilsa has lost something by being forced to stay with her husband. And, as Bergman plays her role, what she loses is the passion Rick once brought to her life. Were Victor fundamentally the same as the man Ilsa

loses, the romantic thrust of the conclusion would be severely diminished.

The outstanding work of *Casablanca's* three principals is mirrored in the performances of the supporting cast. Each actor offers his or her own little treasures to the audience. There is a wealth of nuance in the way Sydney Greenstreet's eyes change depending upon whom he is playing with—they are small and beady when he is offering to help Rick unload the exit visas, wide and almost innocent as he deals with the Laszlos. Equally valuable are: Peter Lorre's sublime cringing when Ugarte asks, "Rick, I hope you are more impressed with me now, huh?"; the strength with which Dooley Wilson gets Rick on the Paris train; the way Conrad Veidt nonchalantly coughs after Renault says he was with the Americans "when they 'blundered' into Berlin in 1918"; the heartfelt reading Joy Page as Annina gives to "He [Jan] is such a boy. In many ways I am so much older than he is"—a

Some recent historians have suggested that Michael Curtiz and Humphrey Bogart always knew what the film's ending would be, but kept that knowledge from Ingrid Bergman so that she would not do anything to give it away during her earlier scenes with Rick and Victor. This theory does not, however, jibe with the writers' memories.

moment that clarifies once and for all her own character's youth and innocence; and the inflection S. Z. Sakall uses when two of his friends mangle the English language, and he remarks, "You will get along beautifully in America."

But the best supporting role in the film is played by, arguably, the picture's best actor—Claude Rains. As was mentioned earlier, Julius and Philip Esptein wrote the role with Rains in mind, giving the character comic lines and bits they knew the actor could play to perfection. When Howard Koch took over the script, he saw the plot's development less in terms of the romance between Rick and Ilsa than the shifting relationship between the café owner and the police captain. In both cases, Rains more than justified the writers' trust in him.

Throughout, Rains raises fence-straddling to a high art, often deliberately underplaying his most seditious remarks. When Strasser tells Victor that all he has to do is provide the names of his fellow resistance leaders and, "you will have your visa in the morning." Rains throws away the next line, "And the honor of having

served the Third Reich!" a clear, yet innocently stated, indication of his contempt for Strasser's method of dealing with the Laszlos.

Rains allows Renault's enthusiasm to show through when he discusses his romantic conquests and when he indulges in verbal sparring with Rick. The former, of course, helps set up his character's identity as "a poor, corrupt official," while also making it clear why he is so willing to shift with the wind. His payoff is his position of authority—and he can obtain that from whomever is in power.

Coupled with his friendship for Rick, Renault's womanizing provides an added source of tension as the film moves towards its conclusion. Will Renault protect the status quo or side with his friend? All of this tension leads to one of the most dramatic moments in the picture, the pause between Rains's announcement to his men that "Major Strasser's been shot" and his orders to "Round up the usual suspects." What makes the moment work so well is the careful way Rains and the writers have established his character's neutrality.

Rains's wry, almost epicene, portrayal of Renault has been cited by some critics as evidence that the film is actually a carefully masked homosexual love story involving Renault and Rick. Although such a reading is not necessarily inconsistent with the evidence on screen, there is no proof that anyone intended to bury that meaning in the film. Given the chaotic nature of *Casablanca*'s production, it is amazing that the film contains any consistent overt messages, much less any covert statements.

In truth, Rains's performance is in the long-standing tradition of the continental lovers played by such actors as Charles Boyer, George Sanders, and Francis Lederer. To argue that Renault is not an obvious "man's man" in the style of a John Wayne, a Gary Cooper, or even a Humphrey Bogart, could even be seen as apply-

In his first scene in CASABLANCA, Claude Rains (right with Conrad Veidt, as Major Strasser, left) skillfully established his character's moral ambivalence by imbuing a simple line like, "You may find the climate of Casablanca a trifle warm, Major," with deeper meanings.

ing the most destructive form of stereotyping to the film. In fact, Renault's approach to sexuality provides a contrast to Rick's that is as important as the contrast between Rick and Victor. The fact that life—and sex—come cheap in Casablanca offers tremendous opportunities to any man in authority, whether he is the captain of police or the proprietor of the city's most successful café. That Renault does not hesitate to take advantage of his position points up the fact that Rick rarely indulges himself. Despite the references to his brief affair with Yvonne, Rick's heart seems to be devoted to his one great love, Ilsa.

Topping the list of the many fine contributions made behind the camera is Michael Curtiz's direction. Curtiz has never been given his due as a director, largely because he was always too much of a company man to earn the respect of critics. During the thirties, the most popular Hollywood directors among the critical fraternity in New York were King Vidor and John Ford, great film artists, certainly, but men who also had a reputation for bucking the system.

Curtiz, on the other hand, did his best work within the studio system. He made any kind of film Warners requested—from westerns to swashbucklers to musicals to romances—and completed his work with quiet professionalism. There are definite characteristics to his work—the strong contrasts between light and shadow, the use of props and bit players to clarify the action—but no overwhelming viewpoint. In films like *Casablanca*, *Captain Blood*, and *Mildred Pierce*, there seems to be a strong vein of romanticism, but nothing you can identify as easily as Ford's nostalgia or Hitchcock's perverse sense of the darker shadows lurking beneath innocent exteriors.

In addition, Curtiz never had as much control over the editing of his films as most of the acknowledged great directors. Thus, *Casablanca* is as much stamped with the storytelling sensibility of Hal Wallis—who sent copious notes to editor Owen Marks—as Curtiz, even though the director was on the set calling the shots during every day of filming.

It is not always easy to tell who was responsible for some of the film's finest visual moments. Was it Curtiz or Wallis who saw the wisdom of using mostly closeups during Rick's first encounter with Ilsa in Casablanca? Who decided to build suspense with a series of reaction shots—from Rick and Jan to Annina to the croupier to Renault—during the scene in which Rick allows Jan to win at the roulette table? And who was behind one of the film's most ingenious uses of montage to clarify the story: the sequence of closeups during the singing of *"La Marseillaise"*?

There are, of course, other sequences that can more easily be credited to Curtiz, sequences

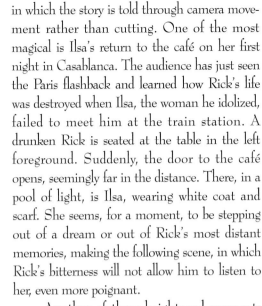

Rick helps Jan Brandel (Helmut Dantine, center) win enough money at roulette to buy exit visas with a commodity less precious than his wife's (Joy Page, right) honor. The roulette scene is one of the best edited sequences in the film, combining shots depicting Jan and Annina's desperation, Renault's concern, Carl's (S. Z. Sakall) realization of what Rick is doing, and the Croupier's (Marcel Dalio) impassive performance of his duties.

in which the story is told through camera movement rather than cutting. One of the most magical is Ilsa's return to the café on her first night in Casablanca. The audience has just seen the Paris flashback and learned how Rick's life was destroyed when Ilsa, the woman he idolized, failed to meet him at the train station. A drunken Rick is seated at the table in the left foreground. Suddenly, the door to the café opens, seemingly far in the distance. There, in a pool of light, is Ilsa, wearing white coat and scarf. She seems, for a moment, to be stepping out of a dream or out of Rick's most distant memories, making the following scene, in which Rick's bitterness will not allow him to listen to her, even more poignant.

Another of these heightened moments occurs a little earlier, as Victor and Ilsa leave the café after their first night there, and Victor asks her what she knows about Rick. They continue walking as she responds with, "Oh, I really can't say, though I saw him quite often in Paris," passing through a shadow as she tells this half-truth. Renault has followed to remind them of their appointment with him the next day. As the Laszlos step out of the frame to get into their cab, the camera stays with Renault, dollying in as he lights a cigarette. His face is made sinister by the matchlight, but his look as he stands there smoking is more ambiguous. Is he concerned that their presence in Casablanca could jeopardize his position with the Germans? Worried about the effect Ilsa's arrival has had on Rick? Jealous? Frightened? Once again, Curtiz's camera movement and the use of light and shadow underline the tensions as the story moves toward the end of its first act.

Of course, the credit for these memorable images needs to be shared with director of photography Arthur Edeson. The film's black-and-white cinematography is one of its greatest assets. *Casablanca* is often cited as an influence on the development of *film noir*, a type of picture that uses harsh, almost stylized contrasts in lighting to complement a story—often a mystery or suspense tale—of a world gone mad in which nobody can be trusted. It is easy to see the similarities. There is a great deal of emphasis on light and shadow in *Casablanca*'s overall look, while the questions about Ilsa's behavior that remain unanswered for almost three-quarters of the movie suggest the duplicitous dames in such films as *Murder, My Sweet* and *Out of the Past*. In the same vein, Renault's shifting allegiances create the image of a world where morality changes with the wind.

But *Casablanca* has maintained a much broader base of support among audiences than any of the *films noirs* it influenced. As brilliant as some of the lighting is in many of the later films, particularly Nicholas Musuraca's work on *Out of the Past*, the harshness of the contrasts almost divorces the films from reality. Edeson's subtle distinctions are more accessible to general audiences, thus contributing to *Casablanca*'s timelessness.

Also important in this area are Orry-Kelly's costumes. With the exception of a few Moroccan costumes and the performer's outfit worn by Corinna Mura, most of the dresses in *Casablanca* seem remarkably contemporary. The simple look he created for Ilsa has helped keep the film from looking dated. Kelly also contributes to the storytelling with his choice of color for Ilsa's costumes. Every one of her dresses has some white in it, with one exception.

When Ilsa and Victor show up at Rick's Café on their second night in Casablanca, her dress has a paisley pattern that makes it look darker. The impact is not as important when the outfit is first seen, but becomes clear later in the evening, when Ilsa sneaks into Rick's apartment to get the exit visas. At this point, the suspense over Ilsa's true nature and her reason for leaving Rick in Paris is at its peak, a situation underlined by Kelly's departure from her trademark white.

If there is any element of *Casablanca* that does seem dated today, it is Max Steiner's score. Despite his effective variations on "As Time Goes By," particularly when Rick meets Ilsa again for the first time, Steiner underlines

Vichy or Not Vichy

One of Curtiz's greatest talents as a director was his ability to sum up a moment by focusing on a simple object, as when the camera moves from Rick and Ilsa's final kiss during the Paris flashback to reveal that Ilsa has tipped over her wine glass, symbolizing the end of her happy times with Rick.

Perhaps the cleverest use of this device in *Casablanca* occurs at the end, after Renault has let Rick off the hook for shooting Strasser:

> RENAULT: (*Picks up a bottle of Vichy water and opens it*) Well, Rick, you're not only a sentimentalist, but you've become a patriot.
> RICK: Maybe, but it seemed like a good time to start.
> RENAULT: I think perhaps you're right. (*As he pours the water into a glass, Renault sees the Vichy label and quickly drops the bottle into a trash basket, which he then kicks over.*)

Through the treatment of a simple object, a bottle of spring water, Curtiz symbolizes Renault's rejection of Vichy France's appeasement of the German government and his embrace of the Allied cause. But this moment would cause props man Limey Plews no end of trouble.

Vichy water was produced, appropriately enough, in the city of Vichy, the capital of Unoccupied France. With the start of World War II, however, trade in the area's chief export had been suspended. Plews searched everywhere for a bottle of Vichy water, but all his sources had run out a long time ago.

Finally, he contacted the product's former distributors in New York, and they tracked down not just a bottle, but a whole case, possibly the last in the U.S. It was in the basement of the Biltmore Hotel in Los Angeles, approximately thirty minutes from the Warner Bros. lot.

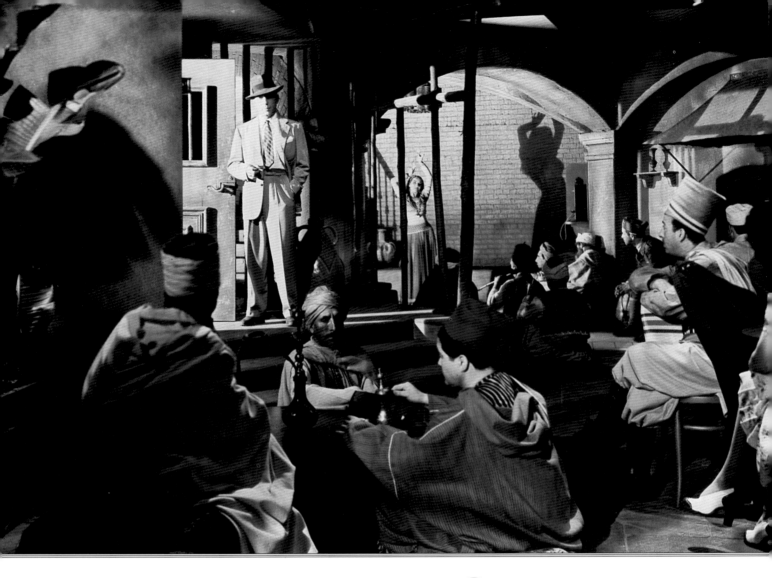

the tension too much with effects that seem overstated, even corny, by today's standards. In addition, he chooses not to use "As Time Goes By" for the film's two most important musical cues: the title theme and the final fade-out. For the former, he uses an African theme that seems canned to contemporary sensibilities. And for *Casablanca*'s finale, he goes back to *"La Marseillaise,"* a fitting underscore for the new alliance between Rick and Renault but something of a let down considering the importance of "As Time Goes By" in the rest of the picture.

But this is a relatively minor complaint about a movie that continues to transport its viewers to another world, even fifty years after its initial release, a movie whose overall professionalism and artistry have made it not only accessible but irresistible through changing times and changing styles in filmmaking.

The visual tension between light and dark helped clarify and intensify CASA-BLANCA's action. The city's moral murkiness was captured perfectly by director Arthur Edeson's lighting of the sets (above, Rick's entrance into the Blue Parrot). Orry-Kelly's costuming for Ingrid Bergman (opposite) helped convey a sense of something purer and nobler by putting the actress in white for almost every one of her scenes.

One sign of *Casablanca*'s continuing appeal is the way different viewers have molded the film to fit their way of looking at the world. The Freudian critic can see the plot in terms of Oedipal conflicts; the student of mythic patterns in literature can relate Rick to such heroes as Odysseus and Achilles; and those of a more political bent have found in the picture an allegory for President Roosevelt's position at the start of World War II (some have even pointed out that "Casablanca" is Spanish for "White House").

The underlying action of *Casablanca*, Rick's move from isolation to involvement, is hardly a new story. Its roots can be traced to Greek mythology, in which Odysseus and Achilles both became heroes of the Trojan War after trying to avoid involvement in the conflict. Later, in the Judeo-Christian tradition, both

Moses and Jesus went through periods of desert isolation before going out to fulfill God's will. The pattern can also be found in Shakespeare: Prince Hamlet hides behind the mask of madness and even spends time with a band of pirates before setting out to avenge his father's death. In more recent retellings, Obi-wan Kenobi comes out of his desert hermitage to turn Luke Skywalker into the next generation of Jedi Knight in *Star Wars*; Tom Cruise's character retreats within himself before saving his country in *Top Gun*; the Man of Steel gives up his powers for love of Lois Lane, only to return to the fray when the Earth is invaded in *Superman II*; and Peter Pan goes through his bondage in civilization before facing the final battle with his greatest enemy in *Hook*.

Some critics have complained that Ilsa's betrayal of Rick in Paris does not provide sufficient motivation for his retreat into isolationism. And if that were all that it took to send him off the deep end, they might be right. The information Koch added about Rick's political background ("In 1935 you ran guns to Ethiopia. In 1936, you fought in Spain on the Loyalists' side.") makes his behavior easier to understand.

Throughout *Casablanca*, the action veers between Rick's political interests and his romantic concerns. The politics keep the story moving, while the romance gives the story heart. Were it simply a film about Rick trying to decide what to do with the exit visas, we probably wouldn't care. Were the focus entirely on the romantic triangle, we probably wouldn't watch. Ironically, this juxtaposition of the political and the romantic is a result of the disputes during filming over what the focus should be.

Of particular note is the way the script peels away layers from Rick, Renault, and Strasser to make their political inclinations evident. Each takes an initial stance that is revealed through the course of the film to be a mere mask. Far from having sold his political soul

for a café in Casablanca, Rick still displays several knee-jerk reactions to the plights of those around him. When Renault informs him that Ugarte is about to be arrested for murder, Rick acts, for one moment, as though he actually might help him, prompting the police chief to throw in, "If you are thinking of warning him, don't put yourself out. He cannot possibly escape." Only then does Rick lay claim to his isolationism: "I stick my neck out for nobody." Later, Rick does indeed stick his neck out, not for Ugarte, but for Jan and Annina, when he rigs the roulette wheel so they can win the money with which to buy exit visas. Following that, he again reveals his true sympathies when he gives the nod to his orchestra to play "La Marseillaise."

Throughout the action, Renault's position becomes more and more precarious. Far from the jovial quisling he appears at first, Renault gradually reveals the danger of the road he has chosen between the Nazis on one side and his friendly affection for Rick (and, by extension, the American cause) on the other. When Rick first meets Strasser, Renault is almost too quick to reinforce his friend's image of complete neutrality, interrupting the conversation with little remarks like "Ho, diplomatist!" and later assuring the major that "you have nothing to worry about Rick." Later, he apologizes to Rick for the havoc the Vichy police have wrought in searching the café: "I told my men to be especially destructive. You know how that impresses Germans?" Although quick to demean the Nazis to someone he can trust, Renault also will not hesitate to keep them happy.

Perhaps Renault's most revealing moment is the scene in his office in which Rick reveals his plans to run off with Ilsa. Renault knows Rick has the exit visas and fears he will use them to get Victor to Lisbon. Renault is obviously under great pressure from the Germans to resolve the affair. But rather than disclosing this in the dialogue the writers (or possibly Michael Curtiz or Claude Rains) reveal the tension through a surprising character

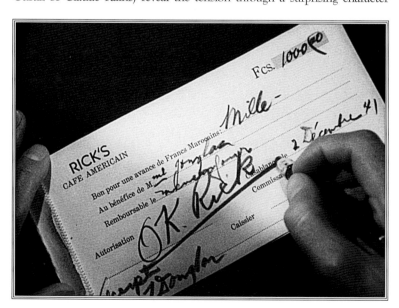

ABOVE: As simple a gesture as the way Ugarte (above) lights his cigarette could be repeated by Renault (top) in a later scene to clarify the film's action. LEFT: The first the audience sees of Rick in CASABLANCA is this shot of his hand, which follows several references to the character that skillfully establish his importance to life in the city. OPPOSITE: The white tuxedo and ever-present cigarette are two elements that helped shape the image of Rick Blaine— and Humphrey Bogart.

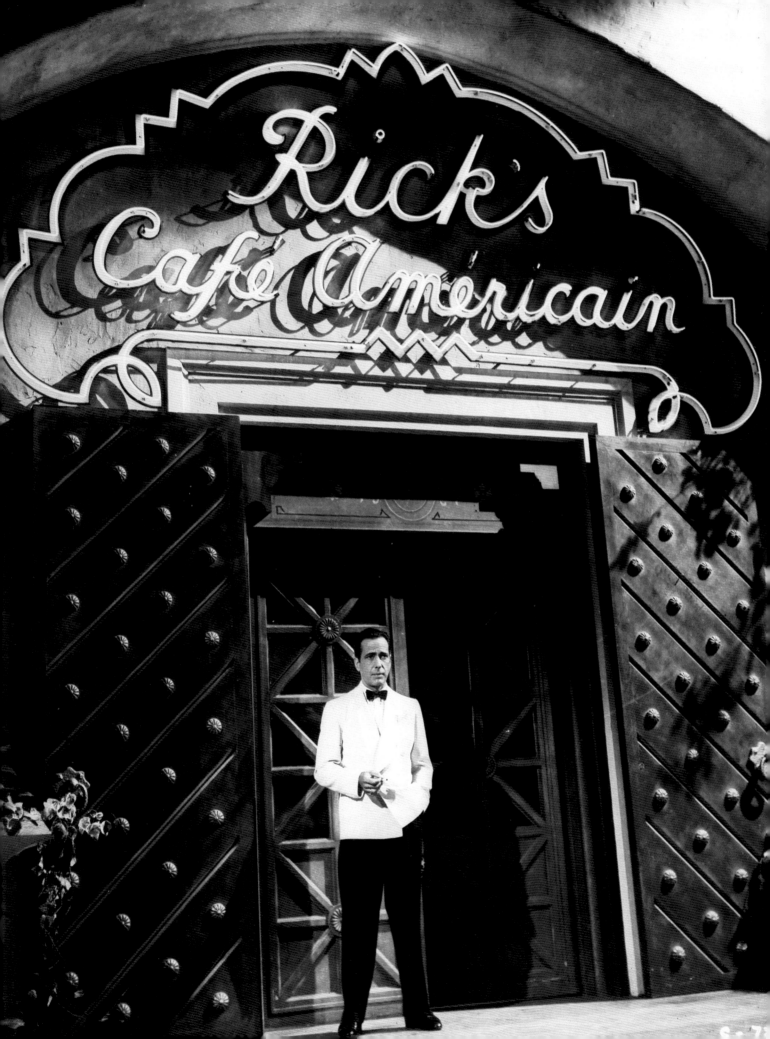

bit—the seemingly unflappable police chief chain smokes relentlessly through the scene, even lighting one cigarette off another. The only other character to do this in the film is Ugarte, shortly before he is arrested and sent to his death.

Strasser's true political heart is also revealed. The character is firmly cast in the mold of most of Conrad Veidt's Nazi villains. At first, he is almost charming with Victor, Ilsa, Rick, and Renault, reassuring Rick that he will not broadcast the news of his background and pleasantly offering the Laszlos a way to get out of Casablanca. By the second night in Rick's Café, however, he baldly demands to know what side Renault is on and, after the famous "*Marseillaise*" scene, demands the bar's closing on the grounds that people are having "much too good a time."

The political plot is played out as Rick is trying to deal with his feelings for Ilsa and figure out what hers are for him. The writers maintain dramatic interest by alternating scenes from the romantic story with incidents that challenge Rick's self-proclaimed neutrality, but the two plot skeins come together for the ending. By melding the film's political and romantic aspects, the ending also provides a double dose of fantasy for the audience. Rick's sacrifice of his own happiness in the name of the greater good appeals to the altruism in human nature, and for every person who has ever loved and lost, Rick's choice becomes a supreme moment of self-vindication, proving that romantic loss can be something noble "as time goes by."

Whenever any film maintains its hold on audiences as long as *Casablanca* has, one of the inevitable questions asked is, "Could there ever be a remake?" At first glance, the picture appears to be part of a small group of films considered unassailable: *Gone With the Wind*, *Citizen Kane*, *Casablanca*, and *The Wizard of Oz*. Even if one could remake it well, the controversy would obscure the new film's merits.

Warner's publicists skillfully used this magazine ad (top) to combine three of CASABLANCA's chief selling points: its established popularity, its timeliness, and its role in making Humphrey Bogart one of Hollywood's biggest stars. The images captured in publicity shots for the film (above and opposite) would make him the screen's quintessential rebel hero, a position that remains unchallenged today.

A new version of *Casablanca* would be hard-pressed to capture the film's original impact. For one thing, how could anyone ever duplicate the effectiveness of releasing the picture as its setting was filling history-making headlines? Even with a shift in locale (say, moving the story to Hong Kong on the eve of its return to China), would there be too much competition from television journalism?

And transplanting *Casablanca* to a different era would eliminate another element of its continuing appeal—the simplicity of the film's moral questions. Even from the vantage point of fifty years later, World War II holds a place in the public consciousness as "the last good war." The villains seemed and still seem irredeemably wrong; the heroes, indisputably right. As a result, no shift in global politics can dim *Casablanca*'s luster.

In fact, at the height of the Vietnam War— a period during which the U.S. was torn apart by conflicting moral codes, and many questioned the validity of any military action—*Casablanca* actually grew in popularity. If anything, it provided a welcome respite from the furor of the times, a return to an era when everything seemed simpler.

Who would be cast in the remake? What could Al Pacino bring to Rick? Could Glenn Close recapture the magic Ingrid Bergman created as Ilsa? What could Simon Callow or Derek Jacobi

Although Paul Henreid is the one actor in CASABLANCA whose work is most consistently criticized, the quiet strength with which he portrays Victor Laszlo plays an important role in strengthening the film's romantic conflict. The one sequence that shows the character's full strength is his leading of "La Marseillaise" and the reaction to the anthem (below).

do with a character like Renault? The speculation could, and most certainly would, go on and on.

In filming *Casablanca* today, the first character who would have to be changed would be Sam. As forward-thinking as his characterization may have been in 1942, it seems sadly stereotyped today. It also would help if he didn't vanish three-quarters of the way through the film. But the problems with that character are relatively easily solved.

The real problem with the story would be Ilsa. Just how happy would modern audiences—particularly the people who flocked to see *Thelma and Louise*—be with a woman who tells her leading man, even one as capable and magnetic as Rick Blaine, to "do the thinking for both of us"? Ilsa's passivity was practically passé when Ingrid Bergman played the role and only worked in *Casablanca* because of the actress's talents. Just a year later, the type was mercilessly lampooned by Howard Hawks in *To Have and Have Not*. A contemporary Ilsa would have to take a more active role in her fate, but a more active Ilsa would completely change the ending. And then it would not be doing *Casablanca* any more.

One of the reasons films like *Gone With the Wind*, *Citizen Kane*, and *Casablanca* are considered impossible to remake is because they are already so perfectly made in their own terms that there is no point in trying again. This mountain has been climbed. Find other heights to scale.

Even though the world's most vicious villains seem to get away with their crimes almost nightly on the world news, there will always be a refugee trail to North Africa via Hollywood. As long as people still make sacrifices for what they believe in and face down bullies and fall in love; as long as Rick, Ilsa, Victor, Renault, Strasser, Ferrari, Ugarte, and Sam are alive on film and on video; as long as "a kiss is still a kiss," there will always be a place where good wins out over evil and love survives in a world gone mad as the man at the piano sings our favorite love song. We will always have *Casablanca*.

Summer 1938- During a European vacation, playwright Murray Burnett visits a café in the South of France that provides the inspiration for *Everybody Comes to Rick's*.

Summer 1940- Burnett and collaborator Joan Allison write *Everybody Comes to Rick's*.

December 8, 1941- The script for *Everybody Comes to Rick's* arrives at the Warner Bros. Story Department in Los Angeles, having been submitted by Burnett and Allison's agent.

December 11, 1941- Warner Bros. reader Stephen Karnot turns in a favorable report on the play.

December 22, 1941- Warners producer Hal Wallis asks the story department to find out the cost of rights to *Everybody Comes to Rick's*

December 31, 1941- Wallis officially changes the play's title to *Casablanca*.

January 5, 1942- Warner Bros. announces to *The Hollywood Reporter* that Ann Sheridan, Ronald Reagan, and Dennis Morgan will star in *Casablanca*.

January 9, 1942- Wally Kline and Aeneas McKenzie are assigned to write the first draft of *Casablanca*.

January 12, 1942- Burnett and Allison sign a contract giving Warner Bros. all rights to *Everybody Comes to Rick's*.

February 7, 1942- Ann Sheridan and Tamara Toumanova are scheduled to test for the female lead.

February 23, 1942- McKenzie and Kline deliver their final batch of script pages and are taken off the screenplay. Wallis learns that Hedy Lamarr is not available for the female lead.

February 25, 1942- Julius J. and Philip G. Epstein leave for Washington to work on the *Why We Fight* series for director Frank Capra. In their spare time, they will be writing *Casablanca*.

March 16, 1942- The Epsteins return to Warner Bros.

April 1, 1942- Wallis notes that he is trying to arrange a meeting at which the Epsteins will tell David O. Selznick *Casablanca*'s plot in hopes of getting him to loan Warners Ingrid Bergman for the role of Ilsa.

April 2, 1942- The Epsteins submit the first third of their script. Studio head Jack L. Warner suggests casting George Raft as Rick.

April 3, 1942- Wallis informs Warner that Raft is not right for *Casablanca*, which is being shaped for Humphrey Bogart.

April 6, 1942- Howard Koch is assigned to do rewrites on *Casablanca*.

April 9, 1942- Michael Curtiz directs Michelle Morgan in a test for the role of Ilsa.

April 17, 1942- Vincent Sherman directs Jean-Pierre Aumont in a test for the role of Victor.

April 20, 1942- Michael Curtiz directs Dooley Wilson in a test for the role of Sam.

April 24, 1942- Warner Bros. and independent producer David O. Selznick reach an agreement for the studio to borrow Ingrid Bergman to play Ilsa.

May 1, 1942- Wallis agrees to give Paul Henreid co-star billing as Victor.

May 3, 1942- Dooley Wilson is announced to play Sam.

May 11, 1942- Date on uncredited rewrite of first third of script.

May 13, 1942- *Casablanca* is assigned Production No. 410.

May 18, 1942- Date on uncredited draft of second third of script.

May 21, 1942- Date on uncredited draft of final third of script.

May 22, 1942- Conrad Veidt signs to play Major Strasser.

May 25, 1942- *Casablanca* begins shooting with Paris flashback sequences. Casey Robinson starts two weeks of rewrites that will stretch to three-and-a-half weeks.

May 26, 1942- Claude Rains signs to play Louis Renault; Peter Lorre signs to play Ugarte.

May 28, 1942- Shooting moves to Soundstage 8, where Rick's Café has been constructed.

June 1, 1942- New draft of screenplay is distributed, but it is still not the final, approved version.

June 3, 1942- With Paul Henreid still tied up shooting *Now, Voyager*, *Casablanca* crew moves to the train station and Ilsa's Paris apartment.

June 4, 1942- Shooting moves back to Rick's Café.

June 5, 1942- Howard Koch is released from the screenplay.

June 12, 1942- The Epsteins are officially released from the screenplay.

June 15, 1942- S. Z. Sakall signs to play Carl, the headwaiter.

June 24, 1942- Final script is sent out in the evening and almost immediately called back by Jack Warner.

June 25, 1942- Having finally finished *Now, Voyager*, Paul Henreid reports for work on *Casablanca*, starting with scenes set in Rick's Café.

July 1, 1942- The Epsteins return to work on the screenplay.

July 10, 1942- Company moves to Metropolitan Airport to shoot Major Strasser's arrival in Casablanca.

July 11, 1942- Company moves to sets for Renault's office. Max Steiner is assigned to write the score.

July 15, 1942- Company moves to sets for Strasser's office, waiting room at jail, and Strasser's car. Date on first script pages with Rick's "hill of beans" speech.

July 16, 1942- Bergman and Henreid shoot scene in Casablanca hotel room.

July 17, 1942- Company moves to Soundstage 1 to begin shooting final scenes at airport and hangar.

July 23, 1942- Company moves to the Blue Parrot set, refurbished from *The Desert Song*, which is shooting at the same time, a situation delaying the shooting of these scenes until now.

July 27, 1942- Company moves to set for Rick's Casablanca apartment to shoot late-night confrontation between Rick and Ilsa.

July 30, 1942- Company moves to Black Market, another set refurbished from *The Desert Song*.

August 1, 1942- Humphrey Bogart completes his role. Ingrid Bergman learns she has been cast as Maria in *For Whom the Bell Tolls*.

August 3, 1942- Last official day of shooting. Ingrid Bergman and Paul Henreid shoot scenes in Blue Parrot and Black Market.

August 21, 1942- Hal Wallis decides on final line— "Louis, I think this is the beginning of a beautiful friendship"—to be recorded by Humphrey Bogart and played with overhead shot of Rick and Renault walking across the airfield.

August 22, 1942- Michael Curtiz shoots one additional scene for film. The sequence is set at police headquarters and features a bit player as a policeman receiving news of the murder of the German couriers.

September 22, 1942- *Casablanca* is previewed in Huntington Park and Pasadena, California.

November 6, 1942- Hal Wallis suggests to Jack Warner that they find some way to take advantage of the almost daily news reports about Casablanca.

November 8, 1942- Allied forces land in North Africa, triggering the start of their first victory over the Axis in the European theater of war.

November 11, 1942- At the request of the New York office, Wallis orders the shooting of an epilogue depicting Rick and Renault on an Allied ship before the landing in North Africa. David O. Selznick sees *Casablanca* in a preview.

November 12, 1942- Plans for the new epilogue are scrapped.

November 26, 1942- *Casablanca* premieres at the Hollywood Theatre in New York with a special parade in honor of the Free French.

December 18, 1942- The Warner Bros. Publicity Department announces General Charles deGaulle's positive reaction to *Casablanca*.

January 23, 1943- *Casablanca* opens in Los Angeles and goes into general release around the country at about the same time as the Casablanca Conference.

April 17, 1943- A New York gossip column states that David O. Selznick will not allow Ingrid Bergman to appear in a sequel to *Casablanca*.

April 26, 1943- Humphrey Bogart, Ingrid Bergman, and Paul Henreid appear in a radio adaptation of *Casablanca* on CBS.

March 3, 1944- *Casablanca* wins Academy Awards for Best Picture, Director, and Screenplay.

September 27, 1955- ABC premieres a television series based on *Casablanca* but set in the present. It runs one season.

September 2, 1976- Murray Burnett and Joan Allison lose a lawsuit against Nathaniel Benchley for saying in *Bogie* that *Everybody Comes to Rick's* "died before it ever reached Broadway."

July 23, 1977- *TV Guide* straw poll of program directors names *Casablanca* the most popular and frequently shown film on television.

November 17, 1977- American Film Institute poll names *Casablanca* the third-greatest American film of all time, behind *Gone With the Wind* in first place and second-place *Citizen Kane*.

1983- British Film Institute poll names *Casablanca* the best film ever.

April 10, 1983- NBC premieres a television series based on *Casablanca* but set before the film's action. It runs three weeks.

April 3, 1985- Burnett and Allison lose appeal of suit over underlying rights to *Casablanca*.

November 1987- Unauthorized version of film, with happy ending, is shown at the Rio Film Festival.

November 19, 1988- Colorized version of *Casablanca* premieres on TBS SuperStation.

December 16, 1988- C. Itoh & Co., the largest Japanese-based trading company in the world, purchases the piano from *Casablanca* for $154,000.

September 19, 1989- *Casablanca* is among the first twenty-five movies named to the National Film Registry.

PLAY IT,

S a m . P l a y

"AS TIME GOES BY."

When *Casablanca*'s many fans come together, one of the questions most often asked is just how much the film owes to the Murray Burnett–Joan Allison play. In the fifty years since the film premiered, relatively little has been said of the original manuscript, most writers preferring to concentrate on the battles that went into writing, casting, and shooting the screenplay.

In some cases, circumstances have actually tended to obscure the importance of the original play. Howard Koch, one of the three writers credited with the *Casablanca* script, never even saw the original, working entirely from earlier drafts of the screenplay. As a result, he tended to downplay its importance when asked in later years about the film's success. It wasn't until 1991, when Burnett complained to *The Los Angeles Times* about this oversight, that Koch set the record straight with an apology.

Other writers over the years have firmly stated that *Casablanca* is one of the few classic films to have an original script, while Humphrey Bogart's biographer, Nathaniel Benchley, stated that the play "died before it ever reached Broadway," a remark that elicited an unsuccessful libel suit from Burnett and Allison. Even at the time of *Casablanca*'s release, the play was given short shrift. Critic James Agee wrote in *The Nation* that the film was "obviously an improvement on one of the world's worst plays," but how he developed that value judgment is anybody's guess, because the script was not produced for the stage until 1946 in Rhode Island.

By no critical standard would *Everybody Comes to Rick's* be considered a great play, but neither is it a total failure. And whatever one may think of the script, it is impossible to deny the similarities it bears to the final film in lines, characters, plot elements, even entire scenes.

In 1937, Murray Burnett was a twenty-six-year-old aspiring playwright earning a living as a vocational-school teacher. For his first venture, he put together a play about—what else?—the life of a vocational-school teacher. While working on *An Apple for the Teacher*, he met a young woman named Joan Allison who had theatrical ambitions of her own. She introduced him to a producer friend of hers who, much to Burnett's surprise, optioned the work-in-progress. The producer urged Burnett and Allison to work on a new draft, which apparently did

not work out, and the play's option lapsed.

Then, Burnett and his wife decided to take a vacation during the summer of 1938. With Germany's continuing military buildup, Mrs. Burnett was worried about the fate of her family members living in Austria, which the Third Reich had recently annexed. Burnett and his wife wanted to witness the Nazi occupation first hand.

In Vienna, Burnett learned about the refugee trail—from Marseilles to Morocco to Lisbon and thence to America—that would become a key part of *Everybody Comes to Rick's*. There was little he and his wife could do for her Austrian relations, however, so they traveled on to the South of France. There, he visited a small café where a black singer-piano player was drawing crowds of people of all nationalities, many of them just starting their journeys as refugees. Equally intriguing was the star of the show, a black American who had wound up on the French Riviera. Like any good playwright, Burnett started asking himself: How did this man get here? What will happen to all these people? How did such a disparate audience come together in the first place? He turned to his wife and said, "You know, this would make a really terrific setting for a play."

First, though, following their return to New York, Burnett and Allison worked on a piece titled *One in a Million*. They were determined to expose the Nazi menace through a spy story. The finished script attracted the attention of Viennese-born director Otto Preminger, who was horrified at what the Germans were doing to his homeland and his fellow Jews, and was looking for an anti-Nazi project. But even as their meetings with Preminger progressed, Burnett and Allison were developing a stronger interest in another play inspired by the European trip. When the Preminger production was eventually cancelled, the couple had their next project in mind.

Through the summer of 1940, they wrote *Everybody Comes to Rick's*. With the German invasion of France, they decided to move the locale to French Morocco and a city named Casablanca, the last stop on the refugee trail where one could be detained by the Third Reich. The black jazz musician became the employee of a mysterious expatriate American running from a love affair that had soured. The play was set in the main room of the American's bar, Rick's Café.

What's in a Name? Not Much!

Although nobody at Warner Bros. ever questioned the idea of using irrevocable exit visas as the hinge for *Casablanca*'s plot, sometime during the filming of Peter Lorre's scenes, May 28—June 2, somebody realized that Marshal Weygand's signature might not carry much weight with the Vichy government. Weygand had retired in December 1941, the month in which *Casablanca* was set. So a change was made that is not reflected in a single draft of the script. On camera, Ugarte's precious exit visas displayed the signature of General Charles deGaulle. But why German-occupied France would have honored the signature of the Free French leader is anybody's guess.

s the curtain rises on *Everybody Comes to Rick's*, the black entertainer, Sam the Rabbit, is performing for a crowd of varied nationalities. Ugarte—a man of *"about forty, distinguished, with a comforting aura of solidity and dignity about him"*—enters and speaks with Rick. Rick refuses to join Ugarte at his table; he never drinks with the customers. The two are interrupted by a blustering Englishman named Forrester-Smith who complains about not being admitted to the gambling room. Rick states that Forrester-Smith has left a trail of bad checks from Honolulu to Calcutta and says, "You're lucky the bar's still open to you."

The next scene between Rick and Ugarte reveals the theft of two exit visas from a pair of German couriers who were killed in the robbery. Ugarte describes the documents as "Letters of transit signed by [French general] Marshal Weygand. They cannot be rescinded or questioned." The scene also establishes Rick's contempt for Ugarte. ("You remind me of a pimp who's had a windfall. When he quits, he's so sorry for the girls.") Despite his contempt, Rick is the only man Ugarte trusts, so the thief asks him to hold the visas until his customers arrive.

A man in a uniform, Rinaldo, then enters and tells Rick that the famed resistance fighter Victor Laszlo has arrived in Casablanca and is seeking an exit visa. Rick bets Rinaldo 5,000 francs that Laszlo will succeed in getting to Lisbon. Rinaldo informs Rick that Laszlo is traveling with a lady and then discusses Rick's past:

(*He takes a little black book from his pocket, opens it, and riffles through the pages*) Ah, here you are. Richard Blaine, American. Age (here I shall be discreet) formerly a prominent and successful attorney in Paris. Married to the daughter of Alexander Kirby. Two children. Left Paris in 1937 because… (*At this point RICK stiffens, and makes an almost threatening gesture. RINALDO looks at him slyly*) We will pass over that. Your wife obtained her divorce in Reno, in 1939 and has custody of the children.

At this point, Yvonne, *"a striking looking blonde,"* enters and disrupts the scene with her drunken protestations of love for Rick.

In the next scene, Rick is approached by Señor Martinez, the owner of a rival club called the Blue Parrot. Martinez offers to buy Rick's place or at least pick up Sam's contract. Rick calls Sam over to hear Martinez's offer and advises the entertainer that he is free to choose. But even with Martinez's offer to double his salary, the Rabbit declines: "Ah ain't got no time to spend whut ah makes here."

The next character to appear is *"A YOUNG MAN in German uniform…fresh-faced, with a clear healthy complexion, bright blue eyes, and the typical cropped head of the Prussians."* This is Captain Strasser, the new attaché to the German Consulate. Strasser and Rick discuss the war, giving Rick a chance to demonstrate his neutrality when he says his "political opinions do not interfere with the operation of this café. When they do, Captain Strasser, I shall be very glad to answer any questions you may ask."

Strasser then explains his assignment to keep Victor Laszlo from leaving Casablanca:

Victor Laszlo never ceased publishing the foulest lies in his Prague newspapers until the very day we marched in. And even after that, he continues to print scandal sheets in a cellar.…He managed to escape from Prague just as we were closing in. In Paris, he continued his activities with the French press. We almost had him there, but once again he slipped through our hands and we lost all trace of him. Until now!…We shall make certain that he does not leave until he has returned the fortune which is rightfully ours…the money he made spreading lies about the German government.

Ugarte then enters from the gambling room and is taken off by Strasser as Sam calms the crowd by leading them in a group-participation song, "Old Man Mose," and Rick goes to his room above the bar. When the song ends, Victor Laszlo—*"slender, small boned, intense looking, with the face of a poet"*—enters with Lois Meredith. She is described as *"a strikingly beautiful woman, a tall, lissome brunette with startlingly blue eyes and ivory complexion. She wears a magnificent white gown, and a full length cape of the same fabric. Her jewels are fabulous. Her beauty and chic are such that people turn to stare."*

From Rinaldo, Victor learns of Ugarte's arrest. Strasser then explains that Victor will not leave Casablanca unless he turns his fortune over to the German government. Victor refuses and asks Strasser to leave. Then, Lois asks Sam to play a favorite song of hers, "As Time Goes By."

The music brings Rick from his room, but before he can tell Sam to stop, he sees Lois. Breaking a long-time precedent, Rick joins Victor and Lois at their table, prompting Rinaldo to comment, "Madame, you have just made history." Rick and Lois recall their last meeting, at La Belle Aurore in Paris, and Rick slips his apartment key to Lois. The others leave Rick

Playwright Murray Burnett today.

alone with Sam—it's late and the café has been emptying throughout the scene. In an exchange that's very close to the final film, Sam tries to get Rick to go fishing with him to get away from Lois and Victor. Then, Rick takes a drink—his first in the play—and makes an unexpected request, "Sam! Get over to that piano!…Play it, you dumb bastard."

Act 2, Scene 1, opens the next morning. Rick comes down from his apartment, soon followed by Lois, who is dressed in the same gown she wore the night before.

Their reminiscences about the past quickly turn into an argument. Lois marvels that her betrayal turned "Richard Blaine, of Paris, criminal lawyer, champion of lost causes" into "Rick, dispenser of entertainment for Casablanca." He blames her for his transformation: "You fixed that, darling. Remember? You took everything that I ever believed in, swept it up into a neat little pile, and put a match to it. Now it's gone. Burnt out, that's me. No cause to believe in. Nothing to fight for."

Finally, Rick reveals what destroyed their relationship. Although a married man with two children, he conducted a year-long affair with Lois in Paris. She knew he was married, but he did not know that she was being kept by a man named Henri. "And then, on the evening of April twelfth, 1935, you walked into La Belle Aurore. With that perfumed thing that called itself a man." It took Rick four years to get over Lois, but now that they have spent the night together, he is free of her.

Then, Lois explains what their one-night reunion meant to her:

You've told me your little dream. Now listen to mine. A fairy tale with a nasty ending. Once upon a time I met a man in Paris—and there were fireworks. When I looked up at the sky I didn't feel small and all alone—instead I thought I could reach up and touch the stars with my hands.…He left and sometimes I used to dream of what would happen if I ever met him again. And then I did…in a cafe in Morocco…and for a little while I was back in Paris. But I was fooling myself, Rick. When the dawn came I was in Morocco, in a tawdry cafe with a man who was empty of everything except bitterness.

Finally, Rick breaks down and admits he still loves Lois. Sam enters, and the two tell him of their reunion and ask him to play "As

Time Goes By" again. Rick suggests that they go back to America together and reveals that he has the exit visas. But she wants to go back to the hotel to get her things and explain the situation to Victor, to whom she feels she owes her life:

Victor could have been in America by now…if it weren't for me.…I got sick at the wrong time. Victor had every opportunity to get away safely in those last hectic days before the armistice. But he stayed. By the time I was well enough to go, things were so bad that I would never have gotten this far without him. Don't you think that the decent thing to do would be to go back there and tell him?

Rick then informs Lois that Rinaldo and Strasser will make sure that Victor stays in Casablanca. Lois begs Rick to help him, and finally Rick agrees. But then Rinaldo enters:

RINALDO: I have an apology to make to Madam.…You see Rick, I told Madam that you were the most influential man in Casablanca, but I neglected to add that not even you can obtain an exit visa for Victor Laszlo. (LOIS stands as if turned to stone, immobile, white. RICK turns and walks rather unsteadily to the bar and gropes blindly for a bottle. He pours himself a stiff drink)

LOIS: (Through stiff lips) I suppose it's useless.…but I love you, Rick.

RICK: (*Looking at her in the mirror behind the bar*) You bitch!
CURTAIN

Act 2, Scene 2, takes place that evening. The café is crowded with customers. Rinaldo informs Sam that Ugarte is dead and questions him to see if he knows anything about the missing exit visas. Rinaldo then tries to get Rick to admit to possessing the visas. He also informs the café owner that Lois spent the night with him at Victor's urging.

Rinaldo leaves, and Victor enters. Rick accuses Victor of pimping to get the exit visas and refuses to believe his protestations. Lois enters, and Rick suggests she try sleeping with Rinaldo, "who is much more susceptible than I, and I assure you, much more sensible." Rick walks off, and Laszlo assures Lois that he forgives her for anything she might have done the night before.

Two German officers force Sam to accompany their singing of the "*Horst Wessel*," much to the discomfort of Sam and the other customers. When they are finished, Victor approaches Sam and asks him to play "*La Marseillaise*." Rick has been attracted by the noise and nods his approval to Sam. At first Victor sings alone, but before long everyone but the two German officers has joined in.

Rinaldo returns with Jan and Annina Viereck, a young Bulgarian couple eager to get to Lisbon. Rinaldo takes Jan off to the gambling room, and in a scene almost identical to the one in the film, Annina asks Rick's advice about whether or not she should sleep with Rinaldo in return for exit visas.

Rinaldo reenters with Jan, and Rick goes off. Rinaldo tries to ply Annina with champagne, despite Jan's objections. Finally, Rinaldo tires of Jan's interference and informs him that "If you want an exit visa, do not interfere." Rick comes back as Jan takes a swing at Rinaldo. Rick switches off the lights, and when they come back on, Jan and Annina are nowhere to be seen. Knowing Rick is hiding the couple, Rinaldo closes the place. Before everyone can leave, however, Rick assures Lois and Victor that he will call them later. After he is certain Rinaldo has gone, Rick opens a secret panel to reveal Jan and Annina.

As the curtain rises on Act 3, Sam is delivering airplane tickets to Rick. Rinaldo enters and once more demands that Rick turn the Vierecks over to him. On Rinaldo's exit, the couple enters from the gambling room. Jan wants to turn himself in rather than allow Rick to sacrifice any more on their behalf, but Rick

assures them that he will think of something. After some deliberation, he calls Rinaldo on the phone and tells him to "come on over here, and I'll have something that *will* interest you."

There is a knock on the door, and the Vierecks go back to the gambling room to hide. Lois enters and announces that although she originally spent the night with Rick to get the exit visas from him, she now realizes that she still loves him and wants to stay in Casablanca with him. Rick does not believe her, but asks her to help him convince Rinaldo that they are in love. When the police captain arrives, Rick offers to trade him Victor and one of the exit visas in return for the Vierecks' freedom. As Rinaldo listens, Rick calls Victor and tells him to come over for the visas.

Rick summons the Vierecks, gets the exit visas from their hiding place inside the piano, then sends them off to the airport. After calling off the gendarmes standing watch outside the café, Rinaldo goes to the gambling room to hide.

Victor comes in to get the exit visas. But when Rinaldo tries to arrest him, Rick pulls a gun on him, informing Rinaldo that he has lost the game. Rick then informs Lois that she is leaving with Victor:

RICK: (*Sharply*) You're going, Lois.

LOIS: No, no, no! You fool, I'm in love with you again. It's true that I came here for an exit visa, when I saw you, my knees went weak. I'm...

RICK: You're going, Lois. There's nothing here for you. You told me...I'm finished...all burned out...Victor's still fighting, and he needs you, Lois.

LOIS: (*Frantically*) I don't care. I'm...

RICK: Get her out of here, Victor, for God's sake...

VICTOR: (*Pulling her towards door*) Rick, are you sure it's worth it?

RICK: (*Forcefully*) I'm sure...You've got a job to do.

VICTOR: (*Sweeping LOIS with him toward door*) Thank you, Rick, and no matter what you think...*you're* still fighting.

Victor and Lois leave, and Rick keeps his gun on Rinaldo until they hear the Lisbon plane take off. Strasser enters, and Rick surrenders himself to the German officer:

RICK: (*Starts walking slowly towards door*) So long, Sam. I'd go over to the

LEFT: Publicity spread for CASABLANCA in "Movie Story" magazine.
OPPOSITE: In writing about CASABLANCA's creation, Howard Koch inadvertently gave Murray Burnett and Joan Allison's original play short shrift. He would later apologize in a letter to the "Los Angeles Times."

Blue Parrot, if I were you. (*As he passes Rinaldo, who has not moved*)

RINALDO: Why did you do it, Rick?

RICK: (*Pausing*) For the folding money, Luis, for the folding money. You owe me five thousand francs. (*RICK walks out with STRASSER as the CURTAIN FALLS*)

Obviously, there are several striking similarities between *Everybody Comes to Rick's* and *Casablanca*. The film's setting, several characters and relationships, and the basic dramatic structure all have their roots in the original play. More fundamentally, both play and film share the same dramatic movement: Rick's transition from cynical, detached observer of world affairs to an active participant. And, surprisingly, considering the stories about *Casablanca* not having an ending during filming, the play resolves the central romantic triangle in much the same way as does the film.

Many of these similarities also point up the strengths of the play. The atmosphere is well drawn, as is Rick's overall cynical nature, which is enhanced by some solid, hard-edged dialogue. Also evident is Rinaldo's more sophisticated wit and Victor's sincerity. Rick's relationships with Sam and Rinaldo and the use of several minor characters—Ugarte, the English gambler, Yvonne, and Martinez—to help define his character would be repeated in the finished film.

But the play has its weaknesses, too, which, though not severe enough to earn it condemnation as "one of the world's worst plays," would certainly pose some problems. First, the exposition is clumsy. For more than half of the play, the most popular indoor activity in Casablanca appears to be telling people things they know already. As a preface to informing Rick about the exit visas he has acquired, Ugarte tells the café keeper about the refugee trail and Casablanca. After they have spent the night together, Rick tells Lois all about their affair and break-up in Paris, prefacing his account with, "I am going to tell you why you got that key." All of this exposition is more easily handled on film, where narration, flashback, and short scenes set away from the café

present essential information about Rick, his past love affair, and Casablanca.

More serious are the script's occasional lapses in logic. If the Germans want Victor Laszlo's money, there are easier ways to get it than by holding him in Casablanca indefinitely. And even if the Nazis could not arrest Laszlo while he was under the jurisdiction of Unoccupied France, his presence in Casablanca would make simple any kind of "accident" Captain Strasser might arrange, with no embarrassment to the Vichy government. In the film, this problem is solved by providing Victor with something the Germans could not get if he were killed—information about the resistance movement.

Also questionable is the use of the exit visas as a plot device. The existence of such documents—"They cannot be rescinded or questioned"—is highly unlikely. For one thing, Marshal Weygand, the French general who advised his country to surrender to Germany, was hardly in a position to sign such a document. Also, what use would the Vichy government have for a super-visa that could be stolen and, as happens in both play and film, used to get a dangerous subversive out of the country to safety? None, of course, but they did prove extremely useful to Burnett and Allison, who invented the device purely for the purpose of giving the central characters something to negotiate over. The exit visas are the plot's "MacGuffin," an arbitrary element used to motivate the action.

For such a plot device to work, the audience must be kept so busy that it does not have time to question the logic of the plot. MacGuffins are particularly difficult to pull off on stage; intermissions generally give audiences too much time to question such improbabilities. In film, however, the rapid succession of shots and scenes makes it a lot easier to sidetrack the audience, which is just what happens in *Casablanca*.

The biggest problem with the play—and the one that would give the screenwriters the most trouble—is the sexual element. This is not just a question of the script's containing censorable material. Rather, the behavior of Rinaldo, as well as that of Lois and Rick, interferes strongly with audience sympathy.

Rinaldo's practice of making innocent young girls sleep with him in return for exit visas is presented in a decidedly chauvinistic manner:

RICK: Why do you have to pick these kids? There are plenty of good looking sophisticated women around here who know what it's all about, you…

RINALDO: *Pour le sport*, Ricky, *pour le sport*. There is

Casablanca? They'll Play It Forever, Sam

BY HOWARD KOCH

In 1982 an unemployed writer submitted a screenplay titled "Everybody Comes to Rick's" to 217 Hollywood agents as a supposed sample of his work. Most didn't trouble themselves to acknowledge the submission. The 31 agents who did read it rejected it outright with comments to the writer such as "try something that really grabs you." Somehow a script reached the hands of one leading producer who advised the writer that it was not right for films but to try making it into a novel.

The screenplay was *Casablanca* — disguised except for "Rick" in the title, the same characters but with different names, the same action, the same story. One of the most popular films of all time was either rejected or not recognized.

Frequently, I'm invited to talk about the making of *Casablanca* after its screening in colleges and universities. The students chorus the dialogue along with the actors. They know the lines better than I do. After the showings, they take pride in telling me how many times they've seen it — 5, 10, sometimes in the 20's — in competition with each other. Recently at one college, they came up to me with a woman student in tow. She had seen the picture that evening for the first time. She was a curiosity on exhibit.

Yet parading under false colors, *Casablanca* was rejected by leading wheelers and dealers in the motion picture industry of today. Moreover, I suspect this would be equally true for *The Treasure of the Sierra Madre, Sunset Boulevard, Citizen Kane* and other classics of Hollywood's "golden age" if their stories were submitted incognito.

What has changed in movie tastes over the past 30 or 40 years to account for this contradiction between what is revered from the past and what is deemed unsuitable for today's audience by those in a position to decide? I have several theories, all related.

The studio heads who made decisions in the 1930's, 40's and early 50's — such as the Warner brothers, Harry Cohn, Darryl Zanuck — were no angels. They were autocrats whose methods in the highly competitive industry were often ruthless and barely within the law. Yet they had something that is conspicuously absent in the movie moguls of our own day — a paternal pride in the pictures they made.

They kept their eyes on the box office, of course, but, beyond that, they cared. One example comes to mind. I wrote the screenplay for *No Sad Songs for Me* at Columbia, then under the aegis of Harry Cohn. It was on a daring subject — a woman dying of cancer putting her house in order for her family before she dies — not exactly a sure commercial bet. Margaret Sullavan, a superb actress, played the lead, and Rudy Mate directed with taste and sensitivity.

All of us who had a part in its making assembled for its first screening in one of the projection rooms. After it was over, there was a hush. Finally I broke the silence with a suggestion for a couple of minor changes before its release. Harry Cohn turned on me with fury. How dare I want to change anything (when everyone in the room was crying — "except maybe you," forgetting for the moment that I had written it). Cohn loved the film so much he put all the resources of the company behind it, and, while not a blockbuster, it made money. Love and commerce were not incompatible.

Could we imagine that happening today, when productions are fabricated with money from such varied sources as distributors, agents, banks, brokers and an occasional millionaire who wants a fling in the motion picture business? The producer is merely the person who taps all these sources until the venture is financed. The common denominator is money, and the product is no longer leavened with love.

What star can be had? Did his or her last picture make money and, if so, how much? What "hot" director (not what writer) is part of the package offered the money-men? Has the material sufficient blood and gore, enough sex, enough sensationalism? These are the questions asked, and the answers will determine whether or not the picture is made. It will have nothing to do with quality, per se, nor God forbid, with its social or cultural values. Naturally, the bogus *Casablanca* story didn't fulfill all these requirements. The violence was relatively muted, the sex implicit not overt and, worse still, it had ideas — romantic, social, political. Small wonder it was rejected. Yet how many movies made today will be seen over and over again 40 years from now?

True, a few current films with some distinction have managed to run the money-gauntlet successfully, movies with whose characters and problems we can identify. But how few compared with the many that filled the picture palaces of the earlier period. Those select few run forever in the subdivided houses in our shopping malls while the vast majority happily disappear from sight. What is missing today?

There is a clue in one student's observation about *Casablanca*.

"Films like *Casablanca* show you things you really long for," the student said. "There are all those graspable values floating around in the film. It's full of a lost heritage that we can't live."

What did the student mean by "graspable values?" I believe he was referring to those that touch the heart and make us feel good about being part of the human race. Those, to me, are the missing values in most of today's films, which are a reflection of our society as a whole. We conjure up enemies because we are not at peace with ourselves and we live in subconscious fear of the oblivion, individual and en masse, which Samuel Beckett celebrates in his plays.

The heart does not flourish in the huge bomb shelter walled with weapons we have made of our globe. As a corollary, we have "bombed out" the human values we verbally profess, and our films are among the casualties. But I speak only for the decade up to now. Artists of the future will, I hope, come to resurrect those values and re-humanize our films.

Howard Koch was co-writer of the screenplay for Casablanca. *© 1986. Reprinted with permission from* The New York Times.

A kiss is still a kiss: Bogart & Bergman

something that attracts me about these unawakened girls, something that challenges…and after all, what is the harm?

RICK: Remember Muti…the little girl who jumped out of the window?

RINALDO: She was a fool.

RICK: Maybe, but I still…

RINALDO: They are buying something…they must pay for it…and what a pleasant way of paying!

Later, it is the disappearance of Annina that prompts Rinaldo to close Rick's Café, with her return as the condition for the bar's reopening. Of course, it can be argued that as a collaborator with the Third Reich, Rinaldo is not meant to be a sympathetic character. But his relationship with Rick, with its combination of joking cynicism and genuine respect, suggests the character has the potential to move beyond stock villainy.

The play's most serious flaw is the treatment of Rick's relationship with Lois. Her spending the night with him in order to obtain the exit visas is not really the issue. Given the importance of Victor's work and the great debt Lois owes him, her behavior can be justified. The real problem lies with the story of the past Rick and Lois shared in Paris.

The audience is asked to believe that Lois was the great love of Rick's life. Yet after a year together, Rick still had not said a word to his wife about the relationship. For her part, Lois never appears to have had the least qualm about her relationship with a married man, nor had she bothered to break off with Henri, the man who supported her while Rick made it possible for her to "reach up and touch the stars." When Rick reminds her of how he discovered the relationship, her reply is, "You know, had you bothered, I could have explained." When she reminds him that he was, after all, cheating on his wife all along, his only response is "You knew about it. That's more than I did."

Adding to the problem is the depiction of Rick's past. The audience is given no specifics about his history as a "champion of lost causes" but more than enough information about his affair with Lois. Instead of being a lapsed idealist rediscovering his values, Rick seems to be a spoiled whiner discov-

ering how to think of someone besides himself. Of course, the latter approach is a valid dramatic action (compare James Cagney's character in *The Fighting 69th*, Jack Lemmon's in *Mister Roberts*, or Tom Cruise's in *Top Gun*), but the problems of building audience sympathy for such a person are decidedly greater. In fact, it is not until Rick goes out of his way to help Jan and Annina at the end of Act 2 that he does anything sympathetic. Until then, his character moves from the neutral to the downright obnoxious.

For all these weaknesses, however, *Everybody Comes to Rick's* still had enough potential to attract the attention of two Broadway producers. Martin Gabel, the husband of actress Arlene Frances, and his partner, Carly Wharton, optioned the play but spent months worrying over script problems and the authors' inexperience. With Burnett and Allison's approval, they looked for a name playwright to collaborate on revisions. Everyone they approached—including such respected writers as Ben Hecht and Robert E. Sherwood—assured them that the piece did not need major changes. Finally, Wharton voiced her main concern about the script: she was convinced that no audience could sympathize with Lois for sleeping with Rick to get the exit visas. This was one change, however, that the authors would not make. So, the play's option was dropped. Ironically, Lois and Rick's night of passion would be one of the first cuts made in adapting the play to the screen.

Burnett and Allison's agent, Anne Watkins, then suggested sending the script to the major Hollywood studios in hopes of either making an outright sale or getting one of the studios to sign the writers to a contract. The team agreed. Warners story editor Irene Lee came across the script during a trip to New York to scout properties and had a copy sent to the studio in Burbank. In January 1942, Burnett and Allison signed a contract giving Warners complete ownership of *Everybody Comes to Rick's*, not realizing until years later that they had relinquished any claim to what would become one of the most popular motion pictures of all time.

Casablanca's MacGuffin: Exit Visas

In his 1966 interview with director–film critic François Truffaut, Alfred Hitchcock, who used MacGuffins in such films as *The 39 Steps* and *North by Northwest*, explained the source of the term "MacGuffin":

It might be a Scottish name, taken from a story about two men in a train. One man says, "What's that package up there in the baggage rack?"

And the other answers, "Oh, that's a MacGuffin."

The first one asks, "What's a MacGuffin?"

"Well," the other man says, "it's an apparatus for trapping lions in the Scottish Highlands."

The first man says, "But there are no lions in the Scottish Highlands," and the other one answers, "Well then, that's no MacGuffin!" So you see that a MacGuffin is actually nothing at all.

Bibliography

With two exceptions, all citations from Warner Bros. correspondence and scripts are from the University of Southern California's Warner Bros. Collection and are used with the permission of the University of Southern California and Warner Bros. Casey Robinson's notes on the script and the telegrams sent by Jack Warner in response to Hal Wallis's *Los Angeles Daily News* interview come from Rudy Behlmer's *Inside Warner Bros.* and are used by permission of Mr. Behlmer and The Viking Press.

"Appeal on *Casablanca* Fails." *New York Times*. April 4, 1986.

"*Casablanca*." *Showmen's Trade Review*. November 28, 1942.

"*Casablanca*." *Variety*. December 8, 1942.

"*Casablanca* Terrific Hit; *Gorilla* Average Program." *The Hollywood Reporter*. December 8, 1942.

"Hollywood Frame-up." *Playboy*. December 1984.

"New McDonald's Duplicates Cafe in *Casablanca*." *Larchmont Chronicle*. September 1979.

"North African Fads Reflected in Modes." *Seattle Times*. December 20, 1942.

"Reviews: *Casablanca*." *The Film Daily*. November 27, 1942.

Review of *Casablanca*. *New York Herald Tribune*. November 29, 1942.

Anobile, Richard J., ed. *The Film Classics Library: Casablanca*. New York: Darien House, Inc., 1974.

Agee, James. *Agee on Film*, vol. 1. New York: Perigee Books, 1958.

Barnes, Howard. "On the Screen." *New York Herald Tribune*. November 27, 1942.

Behlmer, Rudy. *Behind the Scenes: The Making of …*. Hollywood: Samuel French, 1982.

———. *Inside Warner Bros. (1935-1951)*. New York: Viking, 1985.

———. *Memo from David O. Selznick*. New York: Viking, 1972.

Benchley, Nathaniel. *Humphrey Bogart*. Boston: Little, Brown and Company, 1975.

Bergman, Ingrid, and Alan Burgess. *Ingrid Bergman: My Story*. New York: Delacorte Press, 1981.

Boller, Paul F., Jr., and Ronald L. Davis. *Hollywood Anecdotes*. New York: Ballantine Books, 1987.

Bourget, Jean-Loup. "Michael Curtiz." In *American Directors*, edited by Jean-Pierre Coursodon with Pierre Sauvage, vol. 1. New York: McGraw-Hill, 1983.

Brooks, Louise. *Lulu in Hollywood*. New York: Alfred A. Knopf, 1974.

Clarens, Carlos. "Critics Choice: Ten Great Originals." *American Film*. December 1983.

Cook, Donald A. *A History of Narrative Film*. New York: W. W. Norton, 1990.

Crain, Mary Beth. "Henreid Lights Up and Lets Fly." *Los Angeles Times Calendar*. August 21, 1977.

Crowther, Bosley. "*Casablanca*, with Humphrey Bogart and Ingrid Bergman at Hollywood—*White Cargo* and *Ravaged Earth* Open." *New York Times*. November 29, 1942.

Day, Barry. "The Cult Movies: *Casablanca*." *Films & Filming*. August 1974.

Dean, Paul. "The Car from *Casablanca* Can Be Yours." *Los Angeles Times*. July 11, 1987.

Eastman, John. *Retakes: Behind the Scenes of 500 Classic Movies*. New York: Ballantine Books, 1989.

Farber, Manny. Review of *Casablanca*. December 14, 1942. Reprint. *The New Republic*. December 20, 1982.

Finke, Nikki. "A Piano's Value Soars, as Time Goes By." *Los Angeles Times*. December 17, 1988.

———. "Hollywood's New Gold Rush." *Los Angeles Times*. December 19, 1988.

Finler, Joseph L. *The Hollywood Story*. New York: Crown Publishers, 1988.

Francisco, Robert. *You Must Remember This…The Filming of Casablanca*. Englewood Cliffs, N.J.: Prentice-Hall, 1980.

Gritten, David. "You Must Remember This." *Los Angeles Times*. May 14, 1991.

Harvey, James. *Romantic Comedy in Hollywood, From Lubitsch to Sturges*. New York: Alfred A. Knopf, 1987.

Haver, Ronald. "Finally the Truth about *Casablanca*." *American Film*. June, 1976.

Henreid, Paul, with Julius Fast. *Ladies Man: An Autobiography*. New York: St. Martin's Press, 1984.

Hirschhorn, Clive. *The Warner Bros. Story*. New York: Crown Publishers, 1979.

Katz, Ephraim. *The Film Encyclopedia*. New York: Perigee Books, 1976.

Kilgallen, Dorothy. "Here Comes Mr. Dooley." *Collier's*. February 12, 1944.

Kobal, John. "Collectors Choice: Heavenly Bodies." *American Film*. July-August, 1986.

Koch, Howard. *As Time Goes By: Memoirs of a Writer*. New York: Harcourt Brace Jovanovich, 1979.

———. *Casablanca: Script and Legend*. Woodstock, N.Y.: Overlook Press, 1973.

———. "*Casablanca*? They'll Play It Forever, Sam." *Los Angeles Times*. February 23, 1986.

———. "Setting the Record Straight on *Casablanca*." Letter to *Los Angeles Times*. June 1, 1991.

Lardner, John. "Pre-Eisenhower: The Current Cinema." *The New Yorker*. November 28, 1942.

Leamer, Lawrence. *As Time Goes By: The Life of Ingrid Bergman*. New York: New American Library, 1986.

Lloyd, Ann, ed. *Movies of the Thirties*. London: Orbis Publishing, 1983.

———, and David Robinson, eds. *Movies of the Forties*. London: Orbis Publishing, 1982.

McNeil, Alex. *Total Television*. New York: Penguin Books, 1984.

Margulies, Lee. "*Casablanca*: NBC's Not so Sure It'll Play Again." *Los Angeles Times Calendar*. April 9, 1983.

Mathews, Jack. "Colorization: Beginning to See Possibilities, as Time Goes By." *Los Angeles Times*. November 9, 1988.

———. "Sending *Casablanca* over the Rainbow." *Los Angeles Times*. November 6, 1988.

Middleton, David. "*Casablanca*: The Function of Myth in a Popular Classic." *New Orleans Review*. Spring 1986.

Morrow, Lance. "We'll Always Have *Casablanca*." *Time*. December 27, 1982.

Nash, J. Robert, and Stanley Ralph Ross. *The Motion Picture Guide*. Chicago: Cinebooks, 1985.

Norman, Barry. *The Story of Hollywood*. New York: New American Library, 1987.

Parrish, James Robert, and Leonard De Carl with William T. Leonard and Gregory W. Mank. *Hollywood Players: The Forties*. New Rochelle, N.Y.: Arlington House Publishers, 1976.

Peary, Danny. *Cult Movies*. New York: Delta Books, 1981.

Robertson, Patrick. *The Guinness Book of Movie Facts and Feats*. New York: Guinness Books, 1988.

Rosenzweicz, Sidney. *Casablanca and Other Major Films of Michael Curtiz*. Ann Arbor: University of Michigan Research Press, 1982.

Ross, Chuck. "The Great Script Tease." *American Film*. December 1982.

Sackett, Susan. *The Hollywood Reporter Book of Box Office Hits*. New York: Billboard Books, 1990.

Schatz, Thomas A. *The Genius of the System*. New York: Pantheon Books, 1988.

Schubart, Mark. "Max Steiner Makes a Case for Hollywood Composers." *PM*. August 2, 1943.

Sherman, Eric. "Oral History with Vincent Sherman." 1975. Louis B. Mayer and American Film Institute Film History Project.

Sennett, Ted. *Great Movie Directors*. New York: Harry N. Abrams, 1986.

Soble, Ronald L. "Big Movie's Big Poster Has Big Auction Price." *Los Angeles Times*. December 26, 1985.

Stine, Whitney. *Mother Goddam*. New York: Hawthorn Books, 1974.

Thomas, Bob. *Clown Prince of Hollywood: The Antic Life and Times of Jack L. Warner*. New York: McGraw-Hill, 1990.

Truffaut, François. *Hitchcock*. New York: Simon and Schuster, 1967.

Van Gelder, Peter. *That's Hollywood*. New York: Harper Collins, 1990.

Wallis, Hal, and Charles Higham. *Starmaker*. New York: Macmillan Publishing, 1980.

Wiley, Mason, and Damien Bona. *Inside Oscar: The Unofficial History of the Academy Awards*. New York: Ballantine Books, 1986.

Wittmayer, J. L. "How Van Nuys Became Casablanca." *Fedco Reporter*. July 1989.

Zolotow, Maurice. "Don't Call Me Mr. Casablanca." *Los Angeles*. September 1988.

Notes

NOTE: Unless otherwise indicated, all citations from Warner Bros. correspondence and scripts are from the University of Southern California's Warner Bros. Collection.

p. 10 "conceived in sin and born in travail": Howard Koch, *Casablanca: Script and Legend* (Woodstock: Overlook Press, 1973), p. 3.
p. 11 "the world will always welcome...": Herman Hupfield, "As Time Goes By."
p. 16 "You must remember this": Hupfield, "As Time Goes By."
p. 23 "Why They Don't Make Them...": Chuck Ross, "The Great Script Tease," *American Film*, December 1982, pp. 15–19.
p. 33 "piece of crap...": Eric Sherman, Unpublished Oral History with Vincent Sherman, American Film Institute, Louis B. Mayer Library, p. 149.
p. 33 "It [had] all of the things...": Sherman, Vincent Sherman Oral History, p. 150.
p. 34 "The Warner brothers...": Pare Lorentz quoted in Leslie Halliwell, *Halliwell's Film and Video Guide*, 6th ed. (New York: Scribner's, 1987), p. 210.
p. 51 "very full, rosy, and perfectly modeled": Louise Brooks, *Lulu in Hollywood* (New York: Knopf, 1974), p. 59.
p. 51 "what is usually and mercifully...": Alexander Woollcott quoted in Nathaniel Benchley, *Humphrey Bogart* (Boston: Little, Brown, 1975), p. 30.
p. 56 "played him for a sap": paraphrase of John Huston, *The Maltese Falcon* (Screenplay).
p. 63 "like a fairy": Jack L. Warner quoted in Bob Thomas, *Clown Prince of Hollywood: The Antic Life and Times of Jack L. Warner* (New York: McGraw-Hill, 1990), p. 109.
p. 63 "Who the hell...": Warner quoted in Benchley, p. 112.
p. 63 "I would": Ingrid Bergman quoted in Benchley, p. 112.
p. 66 "We have enough trouble...": Joan Bennett quoted in Laurence Leamer, *As Time Goes By: The Life of Ingrid Bergman* (New York: New American Library, 1986), p. 73.

pp. 70-71 "an underground leader...": Hal Wallis and Charles Higham, *Starmaker* (New York: Macmillan, 1980), p. 90.
p. 97 "When you work with me...": Michael Curtiz quoted in Ronald Haver, "Finally, the Truth About *Casablanca*," *American Film*, June 1976, p. 12.
p. 101 "Pronounced 'purse' ": Perc Westmore quoted in Whitney Stine, *Mother Goddam* (New York: Hawthorn, 1974), p. 21.
p. 117 "her admiration, respect...": Casey Robinson quoted in Rudy Behlmer, *Inside Warner Bros. (1935–1951)* (New York: Viking, 1985), p. 206.
p. 117 "He suspects he has been played...": Robinson quoted in Behlmer, p. 207.
pp. 118 "I would play the beginning...": Robinson quoted in Behlmer, p. 207.
p. 120 *Rick finally got Ilsa*...: Patrick Robertson, *The Guinness Book of Movie Facts and Feats*. (New York: Guinness Books, 1988), p. 175.
p. 134 "I kissed him...": Bergman quoted in Leamer, p. 121
p. 135 "This is the first time...": Mel Baker quoted in Benchley, p. 104.
p. 136 *He may have had*...: Information from Bob Williams interview in Leamer, p. 122.
p. 140 "Don't ask so many questions...": Curtiz quoted in Benchley, p. 105.
p. 140 "Just play it...in between": Curtiz quoted in Leamer, p. 124.
pp. 140 "Just play it day to day...": Curtiz quoted in Benchley, p. 105.
p. 140 "Actors! Actors!...": Curtiz quoted in Benchley, p. 105.
pp. 141 "Weekend actors!...": Curtiz quoted in Robert Francisco, *As Time Goes By: The Making of Casablanca* (Englewood Cliffs, N. J.: Prentice-Hall, 1980) p. 148.
p. 150 "to carry on with the work...": Robinson quoted in Behlmer, p. 207.
p. 154 "poodle, a black poodle": Curtiz quoted in Paul Henreid with Julius Fast, *Ladies Man: An Autobiography* (New York: St. Martin's, 1984), p. 122.
p. 154 "It's very nice, but I want a poodle": Curtiz quoted in Henreid and Fast, p. 122.
p. 154 "I wanted a poodle...": Curtiz quoted in Henreid and Fast, p. 122.

p. 155 "a tinkle in your eye": Curtiz quoted in Francisco, p. 70.
p. 155 "the beating of the native tom thumbs": Curtiz quoted in Leamer, p. 124.
p. 155 "Bring me an empty horse": Curtiz quoted in Thomas, p. 128.
p. 155 "a jingle bells": Curtiz quoted in Francisco, p. 54.
p. 155 "I say something funny...": Curtiz quoted in Francisco, p. 54.
p. 157 "Ingrid, you are Maria!": David O. Selznick quoted in Leamer, p. 128.
p. 158 "You must remember this...": Hupfield.
p. 160 "with absolute breathless silence...": Haver, p. 116.
p. 160 *the composer even grudgingly*...: Mark Schubart, "Max Steiner Makes a Case for Hollywood Composers," *PM*, August 2, 1943.
p. 161 "You must remember this...": Hupfield.
p. 167 "Here is a drama...": "*Casablanca* Terrific Hit: *Gorilla* Average Program," *The Hollywood Reporter*, December 8, 1942.
p. 167 "By a curious quirk...": "*Casablanca*," *Daily Variety*, December 8, 1942.
p. 167 "*Casablanca* will take...": "*Casablanca*," *Variety* [weekly], December 8, 1942.
p. 170 "The Warners here have...": Bosley Crowther, "*Casablanca* With Humphrey Bogart and Ingrid Bergman at Hollywood" *New York Times*, November 27, 1942.
p. 170 "Good writing, a brilliant cast...": Howard Barnes, "On the Screen," *New York Herald Tribune*, November 27, 1942.
p. 170 "melodrama with a capital 'M' ": *Herald Tribune*, November 29, 1942.
p. 170 "moving if at times slushy": Untitled Review, *New York Herald Tribune*, November 29, 1942.
p. 170 "sin and local color of *Algiers*": Phillip Hartung quoted in David Middleton, "*Casablanca*: The Function of Myth in a Popular Classic, *New Orleans Review*, Spring 1986, p. 13.
p. 170 "Even though the armed forces...": David Lardner, "Pre-Eisenhower: The Current Cinema," *The New Yorker*, November 28, 1942.
p. 170 "not quite up to...": Lardner.

p. 170 "working up a rather serious reputation...": James Agee, in *Agee on Film*, vol. 1 (New York: Perigee, 1958), p. 29.
p. 170 "Curtiz still has...": Agee, p. 29.
p. 172 "So many times...": Curtiz quoted in Francisco, p. 198.
p. 172 "*Daily Variety* had a simple...": information from Mason Wiley and Damien Bona, *Inside Oscar: The Unofficial History of the Academy Awards* (New York: Ballantine, 1986), p. 189.
p. 173 "I happened to be one": Warner quoted in Behlmer, p. 233.
p. 173 "definitely take legal action...": Warner quoted in Behlmer, p. 233.
p. 174 "I didn't do anything...": Humphrey Bogart quoted in Benchley, p. 112.
p. 177 "What a good movie that was!": Bergman quoted in Richard J. Anobile, *The Film Classics Library: Casablanca* (New York: Darien House, 1974), p. 6.
p. 179 "Well, I'm sixty six...": Harold Gast and Steven Gethers, *A Woman Called Golda* (Teleplay).
p. 186 "in full color...": Charlie Haas, *Gremlins 2: The New Batch* (Screenplay).
p. 187 "You probably have the right...": Groucho Marx, quoted in Paul F. Boller, Jr., and Ronald L. Davis, *Hollywood Anecdotes* (New York: Ballantine, 1987), p. 221.
p. 187 "Harpo marries a hotel detective...": Marx quoted in Boller and Davis, p. 221.
p. 188 "I waited my whole life...": Woody Allen, *Play It Again, Sam* (New York: Random House, 1969), p. 84.
p. 209 "died before it ever reached Broadway": Benchley, p. 101.
p. 212 "died before it ever reached Broadway": Benchley, p. 101.
p. 212 "obviously an improvement...": *Agee on Film*, p. 29.
p. 212 "You know, this would make...": Murray Burnett quoted in Francisco, p. 38.
p. 216 "one of the world's worst plays": Agee, p. 29.
p. 216 "It might be a Scottish name...": Alfred Hitchcock quoted in François Truffaut, *Hitchcock* (New York: Simon and Schuster, 1967), pp. 98.

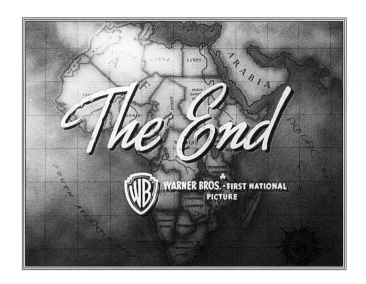

The majority of photographs in this book are courtesy of Turner Entertainment Company, George Eastman House, Warner Bros., Margaret Herrick Library of the Academy of Motion Picture Arts and Sciences, State Historical Society of Wisconsin Iconographic collections. Institutional credits: Copyright Academy of Motion Picture Arts and Sciences—Title page poster spread, upper right; pp. 30-33; p. 41; 52-53, CRADLE SNATCHERS; pp. 60-61; p. 100, Westmore; p. 101, Orry-Kelly; p. 104, publicity shots; p. 110, Koch; p. 111, Curtiz; pp. 160-161, sheet music (cover); p. 172, Jack Warner. CASABLANCA lobby cards courtesy of Margaret Herrick Library, Academy of Motion Picture Arts and Sciences—p. 5, one-sheet; p. 7; p. 22, upper left, bottom. Courtesy of Paramount Pictures—p. 67, Vera Zorina (bottom left); p. 181, ROPE OF SAND; pp. 188-189, PLAY IT AGAIN, SAM (1972). Courtesy of USC Cinema-Television Library's Archive of Performing Arts—pp. 38, 100, 106, 170, *Warner Club News*. Warner Bros. Archives at University of Southern California—p. 30, name change memo ; p. 35, Shooting SERGEANT YORK; p. 43, Jack Warner cartoon; p. 89, Inter-office memo about singers; p. 111, Academy Award newspaper; p. 118, Casey Robinson photo; p. 125, NOW, VOYAGER set; pp. 126-127, four set stills; p. 128, plane drawing blueprint, matte printing; p. 132, lighting memo, Montmartre composite still; p. 134, Paris street set; p. 140, memo; pp. 144-145, set still of Rick's office, drawing of Rick's Café front, and sign drawing; p. 146, Renault's office, Strasser's office, and Renault maps; pp. 148-149, airport sets; p. 192. Jack Warner collection at University of Southern California—p. 100, p. 104, Max Steiner score; p. 106. Warner Bros. TV International—p. 184, "Casablanca" television show (1983). Individual credits: ABC Television (current owner) and David O. Selznick (original producer and distributor)— p. 64, INTERMEZZO: A LOVE STORY (1939). Woolsey Ackerman—Title page poster spread, middle left top; pp. 20-21, French card; p. 63; p.141, right; p. 168. Jack Allen—p. 22, *Cinévogue* magazine (middle); Czech program. Courtesy of Murray Burnett— p. 213, photo. Camden House Auctioneers Inc.—Title page poster spread, middle left, middle right top; p. 7, Danish poster. Courtesy of *The Detroit Free Press*—p. 179, cartoon (bottom). Julius Epstein—p. 42, top. Courtesy of Howard Koch—p. 219, article. Courtesy of Tribune Media Services—p. 179, cartoon (top). Courtesy of *The New Yorker* magazine—p. 179, cartoon (middle). Saul Nirenberg— p. 42, bottom left. Marvin Paige—Title page poster spread, upper left; middle left bottom; lower right; p. 5, background poster; p. 23, French poster (top); p. 39, upper right; p. 96, middle; p. 98, full spread; p. 193, full page; p. 216, upper left. Samuel Goldwyn Company—p. 83, THE CABINET OF DR. CALIGARI (1919). United Artists—p. 187, A NIGHT IN CASABLANCA (1946). Ed Sorel—p. 17, cartoon (left).

Turner Publishing, Inc. wishes to thank all the people "behind the scenes" who helped make this book possible.
Our special thanks to Roger Mayer, Judy Singer at Warner Bros., Susan Tungate and the Turner Legal Department, Jamie Porges, Laura Heald, Beth Hoffman, Carol Farrar-Norton, Kevin D. Smith and everyone at TBS who played a part in bringing *Casablanca: As Time Goes By...* to life.

CASAB